Field Day

Field Day

Getting Society Out of School

Matt Hern

NEW STAR BOOKS

VANCOUVER

2003

Publication of this work is made possible by grants from the Canada Council, the British Columbia Arts Council, and the Department of Canadian Heritage Book Publishing Industry Development Program.

Printed and bound in Canada
First printing, September 2003

New Star Books Ltd.
107 - 3477 Commercial Street
Vancouver, BC   V5N 4E8
www.NewStarBooks.com

NATIONAL LIBRARY OF CANADA CATALOGUING IN PUBLICATION DATA

Hern, Matt, 1968–

Field day: getting society out of school / Matt Hern.

Includes bibliographical references and index.
ISBN 1-55420-002-4
1. Education. 2. Home schooling. 3. Education — Experimental methods.
I. Title.
LB1027.H37 2003   370'.1   C2003-911103-2

To

Ivan Illich (1926–2002)

and

Joe Strummer (1952–2002)

Contents

Preface

You really have to be half nuts to spend much of your life trying to discredit schools, let alone actively encouraging kids to drop out. There is hardly another institution that is so universally deified, lauded, supported and desired. Still, I want you to hear an argument that compulsory schooling should be dissolved, and I am guessing that if you have picked the book up and gotten this far, you are at least a little sympathetic. Or a family member. I appreciate the chance though. Give me a few pages and see if I can engage you in a conversation here.

There is a smallish but vibrant unschooling literature of excellent and often brilliant writing by people like Grace Llewellyn, John Holt and John Taylor Gatto, and I want to add my own set of comments. I want to talk about the idea that transforming schools is centrally about social change, and that deschooling can be about much more than individual autonomy — it can be about social freedom. I want to aggressively respond to a conservative entrenchment of schooling and the continual expansion of a schooled mandate. At the same time, I want to speak directly to the truly incredible explosion of school resisters of all stripes because I think they are among the most powerful forces for fundamental social change.

In a lot of ways this book has emerged out of conversations I have had with classes and audiences over a decade of lecturing, but mostly it is the product of experience, of many years of working with thousands of kids. I first started working with kids because I needed a job, and have kept at it for many good reasons. I have never considered it a career, have never been trained, am not a teacher, have never been certified.

As a teenager I started working at summer camps, then moved to daycares, to group homes, to a detention centre, to running a little free school, to working with a public free school, to running youth trips and now to directing an alternative-to-school centre. Like most everyone else, I have had doubts about deschooling. The longer I keep working and organizing with kids, though, the more I see how kids can thrive outside of school. Children are incredibly resilient for the most part, and many get through school just fine, but so many only really come alive when they are out.

It's not that kids can't survive in school, it's just that they are much more likely to thrive if they are free to fashion themselves and their time. You don't have to go to school to get a job, to get into university, or to succeed — however you might define that. This is absolutely 100 percent true, and the kids around me every day prove it. They can get good jobs, find training, get into college or university, get secondary accreditation, travel and not waste their time on twelve years of petty authority, absurd curricula and clock-watching.

I know this because it is happening all around me. I know from working with hundreds of unschooled kids and my own children, and from the experiences of literally millions of families across the continent. I know that self-government is better than good government, both for neighbourhoods and for children.

Acknowledgments

I celebrate my love for you with a pint of beer and a new
tattoo.   — BILLY BRAGG

I am still holding out hope that I might be a rap star when I grow
up. It is looking a little more unlikely as time goes on, but you
never know. The best I can do right now is give thanks and praise
hip-hop style.

The music I listen to obsessively as I am writing has a way of
working its way into the text. So thanks to Spearhead, Michael
Franti, Common, Black Eyed Peas, Steve Earle, Patra, Gillian
Welch, Zap Mama, Jimmy Cliff, Tribe, Sublime, Merle, The Roots,
Jill Scott, Lauryn Hill, De La Soul, Michelle Shocked, Long Beach
Dub Allstars, Lucinda Williams, Blackalicious, Sonny Rollins,
Brand New Heavies, Roots Manuva, John Prine, Apache Indian,
Shane MacGowan, Speech, Brand Nubians, Asian Dub Founda-
tion, Cornershop, Tom Waits, 2Pac, Jungle Brothers, Mos Def and
Jim Freaking Rome.

Really, though, what I write has everything to do with what's
around me and the people in my life over the past year that I have
been writing this book. Their voices run through it all: Selena and
Sadie and Daisy (constantly), my family on the island, especially
Adi, Pa and Gan, our crew here in East Van: Dan, Sarah, Marcus,

Amanda, Zak, Oscar, Mark, Susan, Levi, Rich, Gli, Stu, Pennie, H-bomb, Sean, Kelly, Kyra, Sam, Elia, Lois, Leni, Anouska, Lucy, Linda, Alicia, Nolan, and Diana and crew. Peace to Stu C. Everybody involved with the Purple Thistle Centre, but really the kids Gen, Jesse, Keith, Lauriel, Desiree, Cole, Mag, Janie, Nate Dawg and Leni, who have stuck with it and worked so hard and had so much faith, even in the face of odds and skepticism.

All the Fort Good Hopers, from both ends, who were so in my mind through much of this book: Mark D, G-Funk, Russ, Marysia, Keely, Bryan, Nina, Ramona, Liza, Susan, Twyla, Lorraine, Junior, Elden, John, Glen, Dave, Muriel, Ronnie, Big Man, Charlie and Laura, Laurence and Patricia and all the families and folks who made it work. Windsor House, Helen, all the staff, parents and kids there over the years.

Everybody at the Institute for Social Ecology, where a good chunk of this was written: Dan, Murray, Claudia, Cuba, Erin, Darini, Brooke, Cindy, Pete, Brian and all who were there the summer of 2002. Certainly thanks to all those who were interviewed for this book and have inspired me over the years: Helen Hughes, Chris Mercogliano, Mary Leue, John Taylor Gatto, Grace Llewellyn and Jerry Mintz. Much gratitude to Rolf, Carolyn and New Star for sure, who had the faith and patience to propose and see this project through.

Some of this book has been published in various forms in journals and magazines over the last couple of years: *Democracy and Nature, Arsenal, Journal of Family Life, Skole, Growing Without Schooling, Social Anarchism, Harbinger* and *Home Education* have all published chunks of what follows.

More than anything, this book is really for all the kids who have worked and hung out with us over the years, travelled so many miles, eaten so many meals, spent so many fun times. Still plenty ahead.

Peace.

M.

Field Day

Introduction

"Yes, but just think how embarrassing it will be for you to be so ignorant. Imagine when you grow up and somebody asks you what the capital of Portugal is and you can't answer!"

"Oh, I can answer all right," said Pippi. "I'll answer like this: 'If you are so bound and determined to find out what the capital of Portugal is, then, for goodness' sakes, write directly to Portugal and ask.'"

"Yes, but don't you think that you would be sorry not to know it yourself?"

"Oh, probably," said Pippi. "No doubt I should lie awake nights and wonder, 'What in the world is the capital of Portugal?' But one can't be having fun all the time," she continued, bending over and standing on her hands for a change. "For that matter, I've been to Lisbon with my papa," she added, still standing upside down, for she could talk that way too.[1]

I acknowledge that arguing against school is swimming upstream in a pretty serious way. Everywhere in the world there is the idea that schooling equals education which equals development which equals prosperity. It is an equation that I want to challenge in its

1. Astrid Lindgren, *Pippi Longstocking* (New York: Puffin, 1977), 40-41.

entirety. In some ways, though, I think questioning schooling is not really all that radical. I know there is a widespread, gut-level response to schools: a belief that it doesn't have to be like this.

At a crasser level, schooling has become a major battleground, and for good reason — it is a huge business. A school monopoly exists, and state bureaucrats, unions and teachers have almost closed the circle. It simply cannot be that warehousing huge groups of children together in packs of thirty, demanding that they stick to a curriculum that neither they nor their teachers created and institutionalizing them for six hours a day, five days a week, ten months a year for twelve straight years is the best we can do.

We need an honest cultural discussion about schools and kids, and a fundamental discussion, one that is willing to look at everything, not just turf wars about money. Right now, conversations about schools have become dominated by a callow two-headed argument favouring mass compulsory schooling.

First are those who wish to see schools deregulated and turned over to the private sector. Typically, these folks want to make schools market-driven and turn over the functioning of schools to corporate, profit-centric interests. Importantly, however, these plans *always* include state and elite direction. U.S. president George W. Bush, for example, is proposing rigorous new national standards, national testing and centralized monitoring of school performance.[2] This is the worst of the worst. It off-loads the responsibility, leaves control in corporate hands, allows for profit-making on the back of social services and refuses to democratize any core power.

On the other hand, we are faced with the advocates for state control of schooling, notably teachers' unions and old-school cen-

---

2. U.S. Department of Education: No Child Left Behind web site <http://www.nclb.gov/start/facts/testing.html>: "Accountability systems gather specific, objective data through tests aligned to standards and use that data to identify strengths and weaknesses in the system . . . The law requires that all schools be held accountable for making sure that every student learns."

tralists. Teachers' unions should be recognized for what they are: advocacy groups for their members. They defend their membership in all ways and typically do it very well. But they are not interested in anything that undermines their fiefdom and aggressively repudiate any attempts at genuine change with platitudes about the undermining of public education. It is a transparently conservative position based on self-interest, and one that repels any proposal to disperse power to families, communities or kids. Asking teachers' unions about schooling is like asking Enron about energy policy.

So we are left with two camps, corporations and government, each interested in maintaining big blocks of power, but the idea that they are the *only* two choices is a dogmatic nightmare. There are other ways to look at kids and communities, and the resignation that what currently exists must necessarily exist is the acid that corrodes visionary thinking, to paraphrase Murray Bookchin.[3] Compulsory schooling has really only been around for 150 years in this part of the world, and already it is collapsing under its own weight. Things can and will change, maybe fast.

To start with, I think these might be four key questions to ask of schools and schooling:

1. Is it possible that the control of schools is best kept at a local level?

2. Is it possible that what one needs to know to grow up right cannot be determined by state bureaucrats?

3. Is it possible that a school (groups divided by age, core curriculum, institutional control, six hours per day, five days a week, twelve years) is not the optimal environment for kids to flourish in?

4. Is it possible that kids and families can direct their own learning (given community resources) in appropriate and reasonable ways?

These are only a few questions, and their answers have to be

3. Murray Bookchin, "The Meaning of Confederalism," *Green Perspectives* 20 (November 1990), 1.

found locally and individually. There is no template for reimagining education and transforming schooling. There are no answers per se. It is poisonous to define what anyone *should* think about learning or how kids grow up best. The idea is to keep insisting that democracy has to be local, that community is where political and economic power must lie and that kids and families are best equipped to make decisions about their own lives.

◎   ◎   ◎

State schooling is among the most entrenched institutions standing in the way of genuine democracy, and it is a massive social monopoly in more ways than one. Homeschooling and alternative schooling are legal, or quasi-legal, across most of North America, but those who do not go to public schools can access only a fraction of the money allocated for them. This puts compulsory schools at such an intense fiscal advantage that typically only families and organizations with significant wealth (for example, Catholic schools) can develop lasting alternatives. Shortage of funding, combined with state regulation and often complex bureaucratic requirements, can make unschooling tricky. Public schools, if not *legally* compulsory, are *functionally* compulsory everywhere. Certainly there are many exceptions, like the more than 1.5 million homeschooling kids in the U.S. alone, plus alternative schoolers, plus uncounted dropouts. But the reality is that school is essentially compulsory from ages six to seventeen and getting around that is a serious and, for most, prohibitive amount of work.

State schools eat more and more public money in the name of education, and justify it in a regressive spending cycle: the worse they perform, the more resources they demand. Education expenditures in the U.S., for example, rose to an estimated high of $700 billion in the 2000–2001 school year. Elementary and secondary schools spent about 60 percent of this total, and college and university spending accounted for the remaining 40 percent. Elementary and secondary schools and colleges and universities spent an estimated 7.1 percent of the U.S. gross domestic product in 2000–2001.[4] There was a historic 132 percent increase in education spending in the U.S. between 1996 and 2003. During the same time defence spending increased 48 percent and health and human services 96 percent.[5] As John Taylor Gatto writes, "Schooling is the largest single employer in the United States, and the largest grantor of contracts next to the Defense Department."[6]

Mass schooling requires the undermining of local control and community power, which globalization eagerly seeks to extinguish. If kids use much of their early lives learning how to function socially, then surely schools are laying the groundwork for a barely democratic society. Centralization of control and the currently vigorous push toward (inter)national standards and testing propel a standardization of knowledge that is happening across the globe. The idea that community-based epistemologies can thrive in a compulsively schooled world is pure naïveté.

The argument that so many progressives and liberals put forward is that state schools are a mess, but that they have to be fixed from the inside. The idea that revolution will come from within is a tired, old apologist idea that carries less and less weight as time goes on. I have no interest in demonizing those who are doing good work in lousy institutions and have no problem with the argument that there are good teachers. I know that there are many genius teachers doing great work, but schools are just not going to transform themselves from within. Change happens and things shift, but schools are not going to put themselves out of business in any significant way. There is just far too much entrenchment of interest.

4. National Center for Education Statistics <http://nces.ed.gov>.
5. U.S. Department of Education: No Child Left Behind web site <http://www.nclb.gov/next/stats/>.
6. John Taylor Gatto, "The Public School Nightmare," in *Deschooling Our Lives*, ed. Matt Hern (Gabriola Island, B.C.: New Society Publishers, 1996), 46.

⊘ ⊘ ⊘

Contemporary theories of teaching have largely developed around the functional necessities of mass schooling, not the other way round. That is, teachers have been forced to develop techniques to cope with what is in front of them, rather than institutions being forced to organize around the way kids learn best. Anyone who has spent any time with children at all can instinctively understand that bunching thirty kids of the same age together every day, all day, is a terrible idea, on every level. Then add in curriculum imperatives — neither teachers nor students have much role in determining the real content of the curriculum — and the overall effect is a culture of bitterness and resentment.

In response, teachers resort to authoritarianism, drugs and technique; kids develop all kinds of crazy psychological, emotional and physical strategies; and parents cope with the fact that they are sending their kids off, every day, to places they hate. How did we end up with this? We are deliberately training our children, from a very young age, to respond quickly and easily to manipulative authority, to change activities at the sound of a bell, to mistrust "learning" and to accept that directing one's own day is a fantasy. There are just better ways to grow up.

It is this culture of schooling that pervades our lives. From the time we are very young we are schooled to accept that learning is synonymous with teaching, and that if we want to learn something we need to be taught. We are happy to trust a one-year-old to learn to speak an intricately complex language like English without being taught, yet somehow we believe that four years later she cannot learn reading, writing, geography or anything else without being taught.

The imposition of a mythological canon, which supposes there is a body of necessary knowledge that everyone needs to know to grow up right, is based on a fallacy that has carried teacher debates for a good two decades now. This canon is the same wall that progressive and conservative educators alike insist on bashing their heads against. The reality is that there is no definitive canon, and constantly trying to manufacture one lays the intellectual groundwork for a universal curriculum and the fantasy of global consumers.

I know there are many commendable things going on in schools today. There are innovative and honourable teachers, administrators and kids all over, but their efforts and good work are *in spite* of the system that surrounds them, not because of it. There are also plausible, reasonable reasons for people to want to go to school, but as author Billy Wimsatt says, "Don't think it's an education."[7] Schools might be useful for some things, but overwhelmingly kids should be out of school as much as possible, and with luck, always.

Ⓞ Ⓞ Ⓞ

Change is going to come. It will (and should) emerge asystematically, locally and from everyday people. Everywhere I go people want to know what they can do in the face of schools, and there are really no solutions per se, nor should there be. Local institutions have to be locally generated because they are constructed in response to unique, induplicable circumstances. The dissolution of state schooling will come about not because some government gave away its power, but because of aggressive resistance, because communities and families and kids grew something else, something better.

In time I believe that schools will be displaced by a patchwork combination of alternatives to school, homeschoolers, resource

---

7. William Upski Wimsatt, *No More Prisons: Urban Life, Homeschooling, Hip-hop Leadership, the Cool Rich Kids Movement, a Hitchhiker's Guide to Community Organizing — and Why Philanthropy is the Greatest Art Form of the 21st Century* (New York: Soft Skull, 1999), 77.

centres, unschoolers,[8] alternative schools and various other places for kids and families to gather. Figuring out how that will come about and what it will look like is the challenge everywhere, but everything is there to build on.

There are kids in every part of the world who are leading great, responsible, amazing lives without wasting the vast bulk of their youth holed up in an institution they want no part of. That is the best place to start thinking about schools.

8. Throughout the book I use the terms *unschool* and *deschool* interchangeably. Occasionally I have heard people try to make a distinction, but I just don't see it.

1 The Politics of Deschooling

"Well now, Pippi, how much do you think eight and four are?"

"Oh, about sixty-seven," hazarded Pippi.

"Of course not," said the teacher. "Eight and four are twelve."

"Well now, really, my dear little woman," said Pippi, "that is carrying things too far. You just said that seven and five are twelve. There should be some rhyme and reason to things even in school. Furthermore, if you are so childishly interested in that foolishness, why don't you sit down in a corner by yourself and do the arithmetic and leave us alone so we can play tag?"[9]

What's In Front of Us

There aren't many issues that people feel so easily and reflexively passionate about as schooling. It might be because virtually all of us have been schooled for big chunks of our lives, or maybe because the fate of children tends to hit close to the heart. It might be that people feel an authority to speak about schools because

9. Lindgren, *Pippi Longstocking*, 53.

they have had so much direct experience with them. Whatever the reasons, I have long noticed just how many people want to talk about schools. Not only parents and kids, but most everyone has a wheelbarrow full of opinions, many of which they are eager and willing to share at the slightest provocation. I think this is an important place to start considering what's in front of us.

Disassembling the whole package and trying to make some sense of a schooled culture is a complicated project, in part because the idea of schooling has entrenched itself so deeply, so easily and so complexly into what we think of as the good life. Ivan Illich describes "school" as "Compulsory attendance in groups of no more than fifty and no less than fifteen, of age-specific cohorts of young people around one person called a teacher, who has more schooling than they."[10] This is a pretty solid definition, and people all over the world describe school in almost identical ways. To say that you are going to school, whether you are five or fifty, is to bask in the warmth of social approval. The answer for marginal- ized communities and developing countries alike is presumed to be more schooling, more education. That schools are a common good is virtually unquestioned, and yet, absurdly, there is also a broad understanding that schools are not benign. It is a truism that kids hate school. There are few institutions that evoke such hostility and antagonism. We have a very strange and confused relationship with schools, a simultaneous deification and contempt.

For me, it comes down to this: Can it be true that children best flourish spending six hours a day, five days a week, ten months a year for twelve consecutive years confined (essentially) to class- rooms? Can it be true that sitting with thirty other kids their own age all day, every day, is a healthy way for children to grow up? Can it be true that constant monitoring, obsessive examinations

10. David Cayley, *Ivan Illich in Conversation* (Concord, Ont.: Anansi, 1992), 66.

and marking, punitive relationships with authority, and national standards develop confident and capable learners?

I think that is exactly what we have in front of us. For more than 150 years in North America schools have been unfettered. They have been given access to every possible funding source. Children have been compelled to attend at risk of dire punishment for them and their families if they resist. Every conceivable social pressure has been requisitioned to the cause. Still, it is a cliché to claim that our school systems are underfunded, that they cannot do their jobs without *more* resources.

My argument is that we do not need more schools or schooling. We need less — a lot less. Not surprisingly, alternatives are all around. Riding shotgun with people's hotly held opinions and critiques of schooling are their ideas and dreams about what could take its place.

@ @ @

Part of the problem in confronting schools is figuring out how to accurately speak of them. Currently schooling, training, education and learning have all become conflated into more or less the same thing. If people take some time to consider the words, they usually make some significant distinctions, but for everyday living those concepts are really all one and the same. That's important because it points to a culture that has grown accustomed to the idea that all learning, all education, all training now takes place within the confines of a state-sanctioned institution. If you want to learn something, you go to school: you go to school to become educated.

The question is, how can we develop alternatives to schools and schooling without reproducing them systematically? There can be no one answer. The blight of state schooling lies in its monopoly and its insistence on globalizing its logic. At the same time, abandoning schools to market forces and leaving the doors open to corporate control is a perilous path to tread. Given the opportunity, dominant social structures always move swiftly to fill cultural or social space, and there are sharks circling, dying to get their hands on all that school money.

Writer and historian Joel Spring speaks well when he says, "Public schools attempt to eliminate poverty by educating children of the poor so they can function within existing social structures. Radical education would attempt to change the social attitudes which support this structure."[11] This is critical to grasping what deschooling is after. Liberals have always argued that mass compulsory schooling will allow poor and marginalized people to fully participate in and benefit from society. Deschooling suggests that schools are vital to creating and building a culture of inequity, and that society cannot be radically transformed until schools are. That transformation has to be a socially ecological one; a locally controlled, radically democratic vision.

More than anything, we do not need mass answers. We need a mass of answers.[12] What we have in front of us is a society more than capable of defining, understanding, communicating and realizing alternatives to schools that answer local needs. There is little question in my mind that there is the will and the capacity and the resources to develop democratic and appropriate institutions to replace schools. The project is to disassemble a culture of schooling and give communities and families the opportunity to comprehend what it means to grow up right and to redefine their ideals of learning.

11. Joel Spring, *A Primer of Libertarian Education* (Montreal: Black Rose, 1975), 9-10.
12. To paraphrase Colin Ward, "Being Local," in *Talking Houses: Ten Lectures by Colin Ward* (London: Freedom Press, 1990), 142.

The Emergence of Compulsory Schooling

The history of the development of Western schooling is a complex and meandering thing, but it is worth looking at in abbreviated form here. A little insight into the logics behind and basis for contemporary compulsory schooling can be very useful.

While young people were grouped together and instructed / trained / initiated into adult life in the very earliest human civilizations, the story of state schooling best begins with Plato (427–347 BC), who laid much of the philosophical and pedagogical framework for schools as we know them in the West. Plato believed that education and schools were the most important function of the state, and that school spending should equal that of the military.

Because schools were so important in Plato's conception of the ideal state, he was adamant that education not be left to private interests, which could not be trusted to keep the good of the whole in mind. He was also clear that once the system was in place, no change could occur. Schools had to maintain strict ideological continuity:

> Those who keep watch over our common wealth must take the greatest care not to overlook the least infraction of the rule against any innovation upon the established system of education.[13]

In *The Republic*, Plato asserted that the state should take responsibility for training children from the age of three and that each citizen could be guided by the system towards an ideal conception of justice and into the social class and occupation best suited for him. Education had to be universalized so that citizens could be effectively screened and placed. In this Plato was emphatic that it was the state's job to support and control schools and to make them

---

13. Robert Thaddeus Fisher, *Classical Utopian Theories of Education* (New York: Bookman, 1963), 35.

compulsory. There was no question in Plato's mind that schools should be designed by the state to support the state.

Throughout Athenian times, though, schools remained largely the province of elites, and the schools, palaestras and institutions of ephebic education were never universalized. The Sophists established numerous schools for teaching public speaking and democratic governance, among other things, but they remained private enterprises. In 600 BC, Solon legislated that every Athenian boy must learn how to swim and read, but even dictates like that were never compulsorized in the manner Plato had in mind. For the last five hundred years BC, Greek and Macedonian culture flourished and spread throughout Eastern Europe and the Mediterranean, and Athenian ideals of education maintained themselves and were widely diffused.

Through the rise of the Roman Empire, Greek conceptions of education remained dominant, though the focus shifted more to literature, sciences, music and dancing while the pedagogy grew more utilitarian. The Romans overwhelmingly left education up to private citizens and independent schools, but a succession of emperors became interested in public education. Monarchs like Hadrian and Marcus Aurelius developed various common school programs that required municipalities to set up schools for the public (largely children of families too poor to attend private institutions) and staff them with physicians, grammarians and Sophists.

As the Roman Empire disintegrated, however, ideals of secular education declined along with it. Education became largely a matter of one's relationship with God, and religious schools in various forms dominated European conceptions of education.

The clerical monopoly of education, established in the age of transition from the ancient world to the modern one, lasted for more than a thousand years, and its effects on the intellectual life of Europe were tremendous. The most obvious result was the general restriction of learning within the boundaries fixed by the church's interests and doctrines:

> But even when the Church had broadened its ideals to permit studies not strictly religious in character or in aim, it frowned persistently on all ventures in philosophy and science which seemed likely to be inconsistent with the central articles of its faith.[14]

Fast forward now through to the 1700s as Enlightenment Europe was emerging from the constraints of religious hegemonies, and many states were making the slow transition from monarchical to republican forms of government. I realize it is a huge chronological leap, but it really is the best place to pick up the threads of educational philosophy and practice that contemporary schooling is built on. For at least a hundred years, since the middle of the 1600s, Platonic ideas about common schools, national education systems and the state's responsibility had been slowly reinvigorated, drifting around Europe and finding particular root in England, France and Prussia.

In France especially, Enlightenment intellectuals of all kinds, from Voltaire to Condorcet to Diderot, many galvanized by Rousseau's *Emile* (1763), began to produce all kinds of comprehensive plans for systematizing national schooling. Among the most influential of these proponents was Louis-René de Caradeuc de La Chalotais who produced a critical text the year after *Emile* was published, an *Essay on National Education*. La Chalotais's interest was in developing a secular system of education to replace the "vice of monasticity" and specifically the Jesuits, against whom he issued a powerful indictment on many levels.

14. William Boyd, *History of Western Education* (New York: Barnes and Noble, 1965), 101.

La Chalotais argued that the state, not the church, should hold the reins of educational power. He also argued that youth should be entrusted to those who hold the state, not God, as the highest authority:

> I am not so unjust as to exclude the clergy altogether . . . but I protest against the exclusion of laymen. I venture to claim for the nation an education which depends only on the State, because it is essentially a matter for the State, because every nation has an inalienable right to instruct its members, because, in a word, the children of the State ought to be brought up by members of the State.[15]

La Chalotais's book had tremendous intellectual influence in France, and his insistence that church hegemony, especially in the case of schools, be definitively replaced with state hegemony both reflected and drove prevailing ideals.

Napoleon was among those who saw the value to the state in controlling schools. He centralized all education bureaucracies and took complete control of education in France, modelling the whole system on his military regime:

> "No one," it was decreed, "may open a school or teach publicly unless he is a member of the imperial university and a graduate of one of its faculties . . ."
>   The university, in fact, was organized like a regiment. The discipline was severe, and the teachers were subject to it as well as the scholars. When a teacher infringed any regulation and incurred censure, he was put under arrest. There was a uniform for all members of the university: a black robe with

---

15. Boyd, *History of Western Education*, 302.

blue palms. The college was a miniature reproduction of the army. Each establishment was divided into companies with sergeants and corporals. Everything was done to the sound of the drum. It was soldiers and not men that were to be made.[16]

Napoleon's schooling system was widely adopted in Prussia following its devastating defeat at the hands of the French army in 1806, and the Jena peace accord left Prussia severely reduced in size and with few resources under its control. Emulating France's success at making national education a state priority, Prussia began to focus on the creation of a compulsory system of state-controlled schools, a process that King Frederick had begun in the 1770s but that had been left incomplete. Among the most widely cited of pivotal points is Johann Fichte's *Address to the German Nation* (1808), in which he laid bare the philosophical underpinnings and practical rationales for monopoly schooling. In essence he argued that Prussia was so humiliatingly defeated because its citizens lacked cohesion, commitment to the nation and willingness to sacrifice for its good:

> The State which introduced universally the national education proposed by us, from the moment that a new generation of youths had passed through it, would need no special army at all, but would have in them an army such as no age has yet seen.[17]

Fichte's point was that schools could and should be used to create a compliant citizenry, one that would be used to following orders, comfortable submitting their will to a larger authority, familiar with hierarchical chains of command and instructed in the virtues of the state.

To that end, Prussian educational theorists devised a model for

16. *Ibid.*
17. Johann Fichte, "Address to the German Nation," quoted in Spring, *A Primer of Libertarian Education*, 19.

schooling built around centrally controlled curricula, constant fragmentation of days into classes that changed at the sound of a bell, obedience and teacher-directed classroom groupings. At the heart of the system was the primacy of the state and the idea that children both belonged to and were the responsibility of the state. As Hegel put it, the state is "the higher authority in respect to which the laws and interests of the family and the civic community are subject and dependent."[18]

By 1819 the ideal of a national system of compulsory schooling was in place, and the Prussian economy and military were booming. Educational theorists from across the Western world came to Prussia to study its schools, and many left as enthusiastic supporters. Among the most eager was Horace Mann, a young American aristocrat who was an education official in Massachusetts, which at that time had a strong network of non-compulsory common schools.[18A]

Inspired by the Prussian example and Jeffersonian egalitarian / self-reliant ideals, Mann spent a dozen years advocating for public schooling, strengthening the Massachusetts schools, expanding their student base, increasing their funding and building their stature. Mann was most interested in universalizing the system and argued that insisting on every child acquiring basic, standardized skills would ensure full-capacity citizenship. He also believed that the continuing rush of immigrants could only be properly assimilated into American culture through a monopoly school system.

In 1852, after years of lobbying by Mann and his colleagues, Massachusetts passed legislation requiring school attendance,

18. Boyd, *History of Western Education*, 351. See also James Mulhern, *A History of Education* (New York: Ronald Press, 1946) and Adolph Eric Meyer, *An Educational History of the Western World* (New York: McGraw Hill, 1965), which are among the better histories I referred to.
18A. It should be said that Mann was really a decent man and in many ways a visionary thinker. The best look at him is an edited collection of his writings and speeches, Lawrence Cremin, ed., *The Republic and the School: Horace Mann on the Education of Free Man* (New York: Teachers College Press, 1957).

establishing mandatory common schools for elementary / junior students in every district and founding teachers' colleges. It was the hole in the dyke, and by the 1880s every state in the Union had passed similar laws. In 1880 the sincerity of the compulsory intent was formalized in Massachusetts, and full enforcement saw the last homeschooling holdouts taken from their parents on Cape Cod and marched to school by state militiamen.

In Canada, a compulsory school system took much longer to implement across the country, was more haphazard in its development and more laxly enforced by the provinces early on. Ontario passed laws in 1871 that required four months of schooling per year from ages seven to twelve, but didn't rigorously enforce it until after World War I. British Columbia had mandatory school laws by 1873. The matter was left to "local option" in Nova Scotia until 1915 and in New Brunswick until 1905. But none of these provinces really pushed the matter much after following Ontario's lead. Neither Quebec nor Newfoundland accepted compulsory education laws until 1943, Quebec defeating two attempts in 1912 and 1919. By the end of World War II, however, schooling was functionally and legally mandatory across Canada.[19]

As Ronald Koetzsch explains, a universal, free and mandatory system was founded on four fundamental assumptions:

1. The state has the responsibility to educate all of its citizens.

2. The state has the right to force all parents to send their children to school.

3. The state has the right to force the entire community — including citizens without school-age children — to support by taxes the education of all children.

4. The state has the right to determine the nature of the education it offers.[20]

19. F. Henry Johnson, *A Brief History of Canadian Education* (Toronto: McGraw Hill, 1968), 70-87.
20. Ronald Koetzsch, *A Handbook of Educational Alternatives* (Boston: Shambhala Publications, 1997), 4.

These assumptions remain intact today and are the political basis for compulsory schooling. The second of those assumptions has come under increasing attack, particularly by advocates for homeschooling, and while it has been conditionally rolled back in some areas, it remains an essential assumption. The fourth of these tenets has also been challenged repeatedly, with less success, and the first and third have never been seriously assailed.

The philosophically Platonic, Prussian-inspired compulsory school system that exists today in North America is the same one that is becoming rapidly globalized in form, function and content.

◎ ◎ ◎

Monopoly schooling did not descend without significant resistance, however. The emergence of universal schooling was necessarily tied to the health and hegemony of the modern state: they are intricately linked. Thus, the most articulate and powerful opposition to schooling has always come from anarchists, three of whom I want to mention briefly here: William Godwin, Leo Tolstoy and Francisco Ferrer.

Godwin is frequently recognized as the first anarchist philosopher. His *Enquiry Concerning Political Justice* (1793) was the first published refutation of the state, and his book *The Enquirer* (1797) was the first published rejection of national schooling. He had tried to open a school in 1783 and when it failed, turned to writing. Godwin believed that compulsory schooling would become an immensely malleable instrument in the hands of government, allowing it to manipulate and affect public opinion for its own uses:

> Before we put so powerful a machine under the direction of
> so ambiguous an agent, it behooves us to consider well what
> it is that we do. Government will not fail to employ it, to
> strengthen its hands, and perpetuate its institutions.[21]

21. William Godwin, *Enquiry Concerning Political Justice and Its Influence*

Godwin's position was that genuine education should be directed towards the veneration and pursuit of truth and justice, but that national schooling would always subordinate those goals to larger political interests:

> Had the scheme of a national education been adopted when despotism was most triumphant, it is not to be believed that it could have for ever stifled the voice of truth. But it would have been the most formidable and profound contrivance for that purpose, that imagination can suggest.[22]

Thus schools were mere tools, and critically influential tools, built for the maintenance and proliferation of state ideologies and patriotism. Godwin's position was particularly interesting because he was married to Mary Wollstonecraft, the writer and feminist, who was a vocal advocate for compulsory schooling, arguing that it would be the best means for nurturing an ethic of equality and allowing equal access for men and women.

Leo Tolstoy, Christian anarchist and celebrated novelist, on the other hand, was more interested in children than writing about them. He established a school for peasant children on his estate, called Yasnaya Polyana, and a journal of the same name which he founded to explore his thinking about schools and children. Tolstoy made a significant differentiation between education and culture, one that I consider striking and still relevant:

> Education is the tendency of one man to make another just like himself. . . . Education is culture under restraint, culture is free. [Education is] when the teaching is forced upon the pupil, and when the instruction is exclusive, that is when only those subjects are taught which the educator regards as necessary.[23]

on Morals and Happiness, quoted in Spring, A Primer of Libertarian Education, 16.
22. Ibid., 18.
23. Leo Tolstoy, "Education and Culture," in Tolstoy on Education, trans.

Tolstoy's school centred on the idea of free inquiry and in many ways foreshadowed Summerhill, the seminal free school in England discussed later on. He held that since teaching and instruction were only means of culture transmission when they were free, students should be left to learn what they wanted to learn, directing both themselves and the kinds of classes they wanted taught. Without compulsion, education was transformed into culture.[24] Tolstoy was less concerned with state schooling, though he opposed it, and more interested in anarchist pedagogy.

Like Tolstoy, Francisco Ferrer was an active anarchist when he opened the Modern School in Spain in 1901. Ferrer was most interested in creating an institution where children could be free of dogmatic ideological interests and could develop in an atmosphere not intended to forge good citizens or religious individuals, or even to instill strong morals. "Since we are not educating for a specific purpose, we cannot determine the capacity or incapacity of the child."[25]

Ferrer was intent upon loosing schools from both hegemonic teaching and state control. At the turn of the twentieth century it was becoming evident that schools were forging not only citizens but also industrial workers, and that government control was essential to the nature of schools:

> They know, better than anyone else that their power is based almost entirely on the school ... [They want schools] not because they hope for the revolution of society through edu-

Leo Wiener (Chicago: University of Chicago Press, 1967).

24. *Tolstoy on Education* is one of the most compelling stories about education I know because it speaks so clearly to the conundrums and ironies of being with kids and learning how to respect and value their decisions. Tolstoy approached each question and instance with such an open heart that he often became mired in confusion. It is his honesty and the lack of historical precedence that I like so much.

25. Francisco Ferrer, *The Origin and Ideals of the Modern School*, quoted in Spring, *A Primer of Libertarian Education*, 45.

26. Francisco Ferrer, "L'ecole rénovée," quoted in Spring, *A Primer of Liber-*

cation, but because they need individuals, workmen, per-
fected instruments of labor to make their industrial enterprises and the capital employed in them profitable ... [They]
have never wanted the uplift of the individual, but his enslave-
ment; and it is perfectly useless to hope for anything but the
school of to-day.[26]

Much like Godwin, Ferrer regarded schools as powerful governmental tools, made all the more dominant by their compulsory
nature. After developing his school, which sparked the rise of the
Modern School movement championed by Emma Goldman
among others and which saw anarchist schools founded all over
the world, Ferrer started the International League for the Rational
Education of Children as well as the journal *L'ecole rénovée*. Ferrer was executed in 1909 for plotting an insurrection against the
Spanish state.

Tolstoy, Godwin and Ferrer were hardly on their own. There
were many from all over Europe and North America who opposed
compulsory schooling right from its first proposal. The resisters
espoused various political stances and rationales, some laudable,
some reprehensible. The point in highlighting these three is to
make clear that the best resistance to compulsory schooling is at
heart also resistance to centralized control, in that alternatives of
all kinds are built on ideals of self-reliance, community control of
resources and local democracy.

Monopoly Schooling

There have really been three core threads of arguments supporting
mandatory national schooling, and they are tied together by a fundamental belief in the primacy of the state. The first is an insistence
that education is a governmental responsibility, not a private

---

26. Francisco Ferrer, "L'ecole rénovée," quoted in Spring, *A Primer of Libertarian Education*, 22-23.

affair. The second is in part an egalitarian argument that if everyone is educated similarly then society becomes a meritocracy. This
line of thinking also holds that schools allow poor and marginalized children a means of escaping class confines. The third argument is that governments need schools to instill dominant ideals
about citizenry in their youth. These are similar to the four rationales for the creation of the system (see previous section) but are
specifically invoked in terms of maintaining a government monopoly. Looming above these philosophical discourses are some rather
crass political arguments about money.

If it can be said that public bodies *should* be responsible for
educating citizens, I am not sure it should extend beyond paying
for it. Further, I am not at all sure that it follows that individuals
should not be responsible for educating themselves. More important, though, are two key questions. First, is the state the level
most worthy of addressing educational questions or is a localized
jurisdiction better positioned? Second, does the impulse to *provide*
educational opportunities extend to making those opportunities
mandatory?[27]

It probably won't come as much of a surprise to you where I
stand on these questions. First, I consider local communities to be
the most appropriate and democratic arena for these questions to
be addressed. The larger state is incapable, for reasons fundamental to its conception, of adequately or ethically driving the institutional needs of people.[28] It is communities that are positioned to
build and develop places that can meet specific local needs and

27. For an even-handed discussion of some of these same issues, though with
very different conclusions, I recommend Walter Feinberg, *Common Schools,
Uncommon Identities: National Unity and Cultural Difference* (New Haven,
Conn.: Yale, 1998).
28. Feinberg identifies the nation as "an imagined community of mutual obli-
gation based on a perception of shared history and meaning" and the state as
"the political instruments for meeting those obligations" (*Common Schools*,
6). I argue that only *real* communities based on *actual* obligations and *actual*

conditions. Educational opportunities are only opportunities at all when they are comprehensible within local social and cultural fabrics and when they are designed to meet local needs. An easy example is schools in rural communities that once allowed students to leave early and/or miss full weeks during harvest time. National standards and bureaucratic mandates now often prevent schools from allowing families that privilege.

More to my point is the shift from governments providing public institutions to making those schools compulsory. I think it is a widely held belief that governing bodies should support a range of public institutions and facilities for collective and individual use, places that are the best of public culture: libraries, community centres, parks, swimming pools, archives. The real question is, why don't we think of schools in the same way and treat them as *utilities*?

Libraries are almost universally regarded as the intellectual hub of the community. They are free, open to everyone, open often and available for any kind of research, reading and listening. There is no qualitative distinction made by the people who run libraries whether you are there to read old comic strips or to investigate particle physics theory. There are librarians available and often willing to go to great lengths to assist patrons, there are numerous research tools from the Internet to microfiche, and there are often meeting rooms, workstations and auditoriums. In general, I consider libraries to be tremendous models for what schools might become. They are devoted to learning and intellectual development, they are non-coercive and they are enduringly popular.

A utility model also underlies the idea that compulsory schooling is not just a question of ethics and politics, but also of efficiency and usefulness. Not only is it wrong to force people to go to school, it doesn't work. People are inherently resistant to being shaped,

shared meanings — mutualities that can only be generated locally, not through the political and military coercion of the state — are ethically placed especially by coercive institutions, and schools are overwhelmingly failing at even their own self-described mandates. A simple fact that points to this is that Massachusetts literacy levels were highest in the years immediately *preceding* the advent of compulsory schooling (95 percent) and have never been as high since.[29]

Other similar figures consistently point to the same phenomenon: more schooling does not necessarily make people smarter, more skillful or more competent, even given schools' own criteria for the most marginal of successes. Despite skyrocketing spending ("even when accounting for inflation, funding has doubled since 1985,"[30]), still "only 32 percent of [American] fourth-graders can read skilfully at grade level"[31] — a figure virtually unchanged in the past thirty years. And of course the percentages in all areas decline sharply for Native Americans, African Americans and Hispanics. Look at the official figures and the numbers will astound you; spending is blowing up, while proficiencies for all ages in all subjects are lower than you could have imagined,[32] time and time again either holding steady or declining.

No one wants to grow up stupid and ignorant. Everyone wants knowledge, skills, information and self-reliance. There is absolutely no need to force people to attend school.

◎ ◎ ◎

The second set of rationales — that compulsory schooling creates a national meritocracy that benefits marginalized families especially, allowing them a legitimate route out of poverty — is one that I address from various angles throughout the book. This

29. Koetzsch, *A Handbook of Educational Alternatives*, 4.
30. U.S. Department of Education: No Child Left Behind web site <http://www.nclb.gov/next/overview/presentation/slide004.html>.
31. *Ibid.*, <http://www.nclb.gov/next/stats>.
32. *Ibid.* Start with these stats and keep going. Truly the numbers are amazing.

rationale requires a careful analysis as it is among the most trenchant and important of arguments in favour of mass schooling.
Specifically in terms of monopolism there are two brief points that
need to be made here.

Firstly, the assumption that poor people need bureaucrats to
make educational decisions for them, for their own good, is a
deeply condescending one. The implication that marginalized people are incapable of making good choices about their children's
upbringing, educational and otherwise, is insulting. Secondly, after
150 years of mass compulsory schooling, among the most radical
and ambitious social experiments ever embarked upon in human
history, the gap between the rich and poor continues to widen,
increasing, for example, in forty-four U.S. states in 2001.[33] Now I
realize that there is a tremendous range of other factors involved in
creating income gaps, but the point is still worthwhile.

Everyday observations, obvious first-hand experience and
relentless statistical data consistently show that poor and minority
students are *not* being assisted by public schools. State schooling is
not giving them the opportunity to rise up out of existing social
conditions; it is entrenching and widening divisions. Even the U.S.
Department of Education's web site has to admit this:

> Since the Elementary and Secondary Education Act first
> passed Congress in 1965, the federal government has spent
> more than $321 billion (in 2002 dollars) to help educate dis-
> advantaged children. Yet nearly forty years later, only 32 per-
> cent of fourth-graders can read skilfully at grade level. Sadly,
> most of the 68 percent who can't read well are minority chil-
> dren and those who live in poverty.[34]

After 150 years and truly staggering amounts of money and public

33. *USA Today* (June 26, 2002), 2.
34. U.S. Department of Education <http://www.nclb.gov/next/stats>.

resources, compulsory schooling is getting demonstrably further from one of its central goals. Somehow, though, school people are allowed to ceaselessly pass off the notion that compulsory schools are social levellers. They are not.

The third philosophical rationale for monopolist schooling is the idea of citizen production. I want to defer the bulk of my comments in this area to several following chapters, but in terms of compulsion it makes for a very odd kind of logic. Do schools reflect or create the kind of world we live in? Either way, what kind of world view are we insinuating by raising our kids in explicitly undemocratic institutions where every decision, every choice is (dis)approved, monitored, supervised and/or graded by government authorities?

What is certain is that schools define a culture that views the most basic aspects of good living as services that can only be provided by others. As Ivan Illich put it:

> Many students, especially those who are poor, intuitively know what schools do for them. They school them to confuse the process and substance. Once these become blurred, a new logic is assumed: the more treatment there is, the better are the results; or escalation leads to success. The pupil is thereby "schooled" to confuse teaching with learning, grade advancement with education, a diploma with competence, and fluency with the ability to say something new. His imagination is "schooled" to accept service in place of value. Medical treatment is mistaken for health care, social work for the improvement of community life, police protection for safety, military poise for national security, the rat race for productive work. Health, learning, dignity, independence, and creative endeavor are defined as little more than the performance of the institutions which claim to serve these ends, and their improvement is made to depend on allocating more resources to the management of hospitals, schools and other agencies in question.[35]

35. Ivan Illich, *Deschooling Society* (New York: Harrow, 1970), 1.

To speak of citizen production in terms of monopolism, then, is to speak of a culture that cyclically seeks to take power from individuals and put it into the hands of institutions and experts. Schools define a need that only they can fulfill, mandate the fulfillment as compulsory, then close the circle by insisting that only certified teachers can dispense "education."

Schools are locked into a regressive funding pattern, with customers guaranteed by law: the worse schools do, the more kids drop out, the more unhappy society becomes, the more money schools demand. Since only schools can educate, citizens become schooled in a way of life that relies on experts for everything and denigrates self-reliance.

$$\odot \quad \odot \quad \odot$$

Over and above all the philosophical arguments supporting the concept of monopoly schooling, however, sit some very crass realities about money and control.

Any discussion of schools is immensely complicated by fiscal realities. Far too many people have far too much entrenched interest to allow reforms that see their money slip away. For example, in British Columbia where I live, each school-age child is allocated approximately $5,300 per year that goes to the school district he or she is enrolled in. There are endlessly complicated funding formulas, but across Canada and the U.S. the numbers generally range between $5,000 and $7,500 per year, per kid.[36] That money is then filtered through a pyramid of administrators, supervisors, superintendents, assistant superintendents and various other layers until it reaches the actual school site. Then it runs through principals, vice-principals, various support staff and counsellors

---

36. "Today, more than $7,000 on average is spent per [American] pupil by local, state and federal taxpayers." Department of Education <http://www.nclb.gov/next/overview/index.html>.

until it reaches the classroom level, a shadow of what it once was:

> Out of every dollar allocated to New York schools 51% is
> removed at the top for system-wide administrative costs.
> Local school districts remove another 5% for direct adminis-
> trative costs. At the school site there is wide latitude concern-
> ing what to do with the remaining 44%. But the average
> school deducts another 12% more for administration and
> supervision, bringing the total deducted from our dollar to 68
> cents. But there are more non-teaching costs in most schools:
> coordinators of all sorts, guidance counsellors, librarians,
> honorary administrators who are relieved of teaching duties
> to do favors for listed administrators . . . under these flexible
> guidelines the 32 cents remaining after three administrative
> levies is dropped in most schools to a quarter, two bits. Out
> of a 7 billion dollar school budget this is a net loss to instruc-
> tion from all other uses equalling 5 1/2 billion dollars.[37]

Consider just how much money is at stake. Here in British Columbia, for example, each school of a thousand students generates a
minimum of $5.5 million of revenue per year. Every kid is worth at
least $63,000 of revenue for his or her twelve school years, not
taking into account inflation.[38] There is an annual budget of $4.8
billion just in this little province of less than four million people on
the edge of the continent.

Is it any wonder that the education establishment is so antagonistic to homeschoolers and deschoolers? What about the estimated 1.5 million homeschoolers in the United States? Is it any

37. John Taylor Gatto quoted in David Guterson, *Why Homeschooling
Makes Sense* (New York: Harcourt Brace Jovanovich, 1992), 137.
38. While each school district receives a little less than $5,500 per kid, not
counting sizable add-ons for rural schools, ESL students, aboriginal students
and disabled students, the Ministry of Education's total slice of tax revenue is
almost exactly $7,000 per child. There were 632,000 students in the B.C.
public school system in 2002, plus 60,000 in independent schools accessing a
total annual ministry budget of approximately $4.8 billion for the 2002–
2003 fiscal year.

wonder that school people are so reflexively antagonistic to any questions about monopolism? Is it any wonder that so many pedagogical arguments are being constructed to justify this degree of access to public money?

Breaking School's Hold

The suggestion that the school monopoly needs to be disassembled resonates across a wide social / political spectrum. So many parents, whatever their pedagogical or philosophical stances, understand what it means to have to send their kid to a school that doesn't represent or reflect many of their core values. I run into people of every conceivable stripe who object to the schools they have been handed. Parents and kids resent the idea that government schools are the only real option for so many.

To speak of school choice, though, is to enter a major melee at the heart of monopolism.[39] Even the strongest proponents of compulsory state schooling acknowledge that building some school choice into systems would enhance flexibility and effectiveness. Particularly over the past twenty years, a wall of reformist proposals has emerged for supporting public school choice, charter schools, community schools, schools within schools, alternative schools, magnet schools and many variations on the voucher theme. The best part of public schooling is the commitment to universal access, but it is an ideal so compromised that even the best intentions have become obscured.

Typically, school choice proposals revolve around maintaining free and compulsory access while building institutional options. The most basic charter school model, for example, allows a group

39. There are many good overviews of the school choice debates, but most are too ideologically clouded and hard to sort through. For a decent basic introduction that is not too obscuring (if already a little dated), try Peter W. Cookson, *School Choice: The Struggle for the Soul of American Education* (New Haven, Conn.: Yale University Press, 1994).

of people (parents, administrators, teachers) to draw up a charter describing a proposed school's character, methods, management and financial plans. They then present it to a specific sponsoring body, usually the school board, and negotiate a contract to access funding. Charter schools are independent legal and governing bodies that receive state funding and, depending on the arrangement, are required to accept a range of applicants, meet local criteria for testing and performance and report regularly to various levels of sponsoring bodies. By doing this they maintain eligibility for public funding while enjoying some of the flexibility of private institutions.

Variations of charter schools, under assorted compromises and regulations, operate all over North America to decidedly mixed reviews. In her discussion of the merits of charter schools, Louann Bierlein offers two representative assessments:

> I believe that charter schools give us a way to be innovative within the public school rubric. They give us a way to move forward on a new notion of a system of public schools. I think that it is an innovation worth trying.
> — *Public school district superintendent, Wisconsin*

> Charter schools are experiments at best and will do little more than take money away from the traditional public school system. There really is no need for such schools since things are generally fine as they are.
> — *Teachers' union leader, Los Angeles*[40]

These are two well-chosen opinions as they accurately portray dominant reformist opinions among public school supporters. Some hold charters to be an innovative way to add flexibility and

---

40. Louann Bierlein, "The Charter School Movement," in *New Schools for A New Century*, eds. Diane Ravitch and Joseph Viteritti (New Haven, Conn.: Yale University Press, 1997), 37-38.

choice to the system, while some believe that they fundamentally distract and undermine the support that existing schools need.

◎ ◎ ◎

Voucher program proposals have been drifting around for more than thirty years now and have emerged as perhaps the primary vehicle for public school reform. In the 1990s, the voucher system was enthusiastically adopted by neo-conservatives and the religious right, as exemplified by Bush's 2001 education plan.[41] The basic model is to provide families with a voucher for each student, worth a certain amount of money and redeemable at the educational facility of their choice. The idea is that families then have some bargaining power to attend schools of their choice, and private institutions and public schools can compete for students on a relatively equal basis.

As with most educational reform movements, the primary impetus for voucher programs has come from religious lobbies, and there are currently several tentative programs in place in the U.S. The most prominent may be in Cleveland, Ohio, where a group of mainly African-American, inner-city parents has been challenging the school board and state in a lengthy political and legal battle. After a series of lower-court losses, the U.S. Supreme Court ruled in 2002 that it was legal to provide limited vouchers for these families to attend religious schools out of their immediate district.[42]

On June 27, 2002, the U.S. Supreme Court, in a 5-4 decision, approved the Cleveland program. At the same time it ruled that "school districts can force the nation's 23 million middle and high

41. U.S. Department of Education web site <http://www.ed.gov>.
42. Joan Biskupic and Tamara Henry, "Church, State Wall is Lowered in Schools," USA Today, June 28, 2002 <http://www.usatoday.com/news/washington/2002/06/28/scotus-cover.htm>.

school students to take drug tests before they join the band, choir, chess club or any other extracurricular activities where they compete with other schools."[43]

Discussions of the case revolved around the Fourth Amendment protecting citizens from "unreasonable search and seizure." The Justices acknowledged this discussion as relevant, but determined that "schools are different because they need to maintain order." Given this victory and the Bush administration's eagerness to push the voucher envelope, there can be little doubt that similar systems will be put in place in the coming years, if only in a very limited sense, and that schools will be further emboldened to pursue their ideals by any means necessary.

Those opposed to voucher proposals point specifically to their free-market tendencies to exacerbate, not alleviate, class and racial inequities. Since wealthy districts already have significant advantages over poorer areas, voucher systems would make the gap bigger, allowing elite schools to attract the best students and teachers, while leaving disadvantaged schools with even fewer resources to work with and only students who were not accepted anywhere else. More than that, vouchers, because their logic is market-based, will pit schools against each other for students, advertising and competing, again allowing privileged areas a further advantage. As Ann Bastian writes, "we are building more lifeboats, not better ships."[44]

I think this line of critique begins to illustrate how voucher proposals are flawed. In a society that is deeply inequitable, a free-market system is not really free at all. The real flaw with both vouchers and charters is that they seek to reform and humanize a

43. Toni Locey, "High Court OKs Drug Testing for Students," *USA Today*, June 28, 2002 <http://www.usatoday.com/news/washington/2002/06/28/scotus-drug-tests.htm>.
44. Ann Bastian, "Is Public School 'Choice' a Viable Alternative?" in *Rethinking Schools: An Agenda for Change*, eds. David Levine *et al.* (New York: New Press, 1995), 205-208.

system that needs fundamental changes, not just cosmetic reforms in the guise of choice. As Joel Spring puts it, "public schooling and radical education are almost contradictory notions ... Public schools can reform and improve but they do not attempt to make basic structural changes."[45] If charters and vouchers were conceived within a radically decentralist context, they might have some potential, but within the current pedagogical and social reality they offer very slim pickings.

The real functions of these and other school choice options are essentially regressive in entrenching class divisions. Further, they off-load all the responsibility to independent projects while the state maintains the core aspects of control. Charter and voucher-recipient schools are required to design and operate their schools, but still have to meet standardized criteria for success. It is only choice in the most limited of senses.

School people are concerned that charter schooling and voucher systems are undermining the essential supports of compulsory schooling, while deschoolers are concerned — and convinced — that they won't.

@   @   @

The only way to speak of schools as social levellers is in the most purely theoretical sense. The vision of schools as fundamentally alleviating poverty by allowing all classes of children a merit-based route to success runs in the face of all evidence, statistical and direct. Schools in poor districts can only be understood "in the context of fiscal crisis and polarized resources."[46] Schooling operates with an assumption of educational scarcity, which schools themselves have created so only they can address it. The claim that school choice proposals will precipitate a vast degree of inequality

45. Spring, *A Primer of Libertarian Education*, 10.
46. Bastian, "Is Public School 'Choice' a Viable Alternative?", 206.

and racial separation between schools is correct in one sense, and laughable in another. Jonathan Kozol, among many others, has documented the almost literally unbelievable disparities currently existing:

> [East St. Louis], which is 98 percent black, has no obstetric services, no regular trash collection and few jobs ... 75 percent of its population lives on welfare of some form ... The biggest employer in the town is public education. Next perhaps is the Pfizer plant, which is situated just behind one of the high schools. After that, the biggest businesses may be the drug trade, funerals and bars and prostitution.[47]

Kozol also talks to a local teacher and football coach who describes the experience of taking students to compete at wealthier schools: "They don't say a lot. They have their faces to the windows, lookin' out. I can't tell what they are thinking. I am hopin' they are saying 'This is something I will give my kids someday.'"[48]

Throughout the book, Kozol visits schools across America, in Chicago, New York, San Antonio and other cities, and documents the stunning poverty he finds. Neighbourhoods and whole small cities, invariably racially segregated, are mired in devastating conditions while white affluence thrives miles or even blocks away.

Visiting schools in these places, Kozol encounters equally crushing conditions. Schools with no windows, no heat, no toilets, flooded gyms, sewage backing up into hallways, too many kids, brutally low salaries, twenty-six textbooks for more than a hundred kids, no way to get rid of garbage, collapsing ceilings, huge classes, regular gang violence, drop-out rates well above 50 percent and many other enormous challenges.[49] Schools mirror the social conditions around them.

47. Jonathan Kozol, *Savage Inequalities: Children in America's Schools* (New York: Crown Publishers, 1991), 7-26.
48. *Ibid.*, 7, 18.
49. *Ibid.* All real circumstances from various sites documented in the book.

One could read a book like *Savage Inequalities* and interpret the stories as a call to government to correct these inequities and, with massive resource infusions, ensure equal institutional opportunity. But when you're in a hole you should stop digging. Schools and the state are inextricably linked and schools are both reflecting and reinforcing a vision of society. As institutions they reinforce the social disparities around them. The idea that wealthier students do better at school while poorer students invariably do worse is a cliché that everyone understands at a very early age. As Kozol incisively writes, "the age-old conflict between liberty and equity is largely non-existent in this setting. The wealthy districts have the first and seldom think about the second, while the very poor have neither."[50]

Radical school reform has to be conceived of as *social* transformation. The point is that programs for "school choice" have little value in and of themselves. Vouchers or charters per se are of little transformative value in their attempt to humanize a system. Schools do not stand outside the present social system, which offers neither freedom nor equity, but are essential to its maintenance.

$$\odot \quad \odot \quad \odot$$

On the other hand, arguments in favour of local control mean little when districts do not have the resources to control anything. Again as Kozol puts it, "if [a school board] has very little money, it has almost no control: or rather it has only negative control. Its freedom is to choose which of the children's needs should be denied."[51] In the overwhelming number of cases, though, it is not that poor districts do not have money; in fact in many places schools are the biggest (often only) industries and employers. It is

50. *Ibid.*, 213.
51. *Ibid.*

that social conditions around them are so devastating, and the children's needs so great, that almost no amount of cash would suffice.

A genuinely transformative alternative to state schooling has to seek not only local control of institutions, but also community control of real resources. The school system that has been so vital to entrenching racial and class divisions has to be disestablished so that municipalities can make genuine decisions about what local children need. The centralized school mandates, the national testing and the standardized curricula must be abandoned.

Schools need to be decompulsorized and school resources must be rigorously municipalized so that local communities can undertake a constant and intense debate about which institutions will provide the best opportunities for all children. The ideal outcome is a basket of locally conceived funding options, offered like utilities that are publicly maintained and independently designed. It is a vision rooted in the faith that people given reasonable opportunity can make rational decisions about their future.

John Taylor Gatto

John Taylor Gatto was born in Monongahela, Pennsylvania, a river town thirty-five miles southeast of Pittsburgh. After college, Gatto worked as a scriptwriter in the film business, was an advertising writer, a taxi driver, a jewellery designer, an ASCAP songwriter and a hotdog vendor before becoming a schoolteacher. During his school-teaching years he also entered the caviar trade, conducted an antiques business, operated a rare book search service and founded Lava Mt. Records.

He was named New York State Teacher of the Year in 1991 after being named New York City Teacher of the Year in 1989, 1990 and 1991. In an op-ed page article in the Wall Street Journal *that appeared that same year, he announced that he was leaving the teaching profession because he was no longer willing to hurt children. Later that year he was the subject of a show at Carnegie Hall called "An Evening With John Taylor Gatto," which launched a career of public speaking in the area of school reform that has taken Gatto over a million and a half miles in all fifty U.S. states and seven foreign countries.*

His books include Dumbing Us Down: The Hidden Curriculum of Compulsory Schooling *(1992);* The Exhausted School *(1993);* A Different Kind of Teacher *(2000); and* The Underground History of American Education *(2001). Gatto is currently at work on a documentary film about the nature of modern schooling entitled* The Fourth Purpose, *with his friend and former student Roland Legiardi-Laura. He has been married for forty years to the same woman and has two grown children and a cat.*

This a partial and (very) condensed[52] transcript of a series of letters Gatto and I exchanged as part of a longer ongoing conversation in 2001.

⊙ ⊙ ⊙

Yo John.

Matt here in East Vancouver. I am putting together a new book. I want to look seriously at the politics of deschooling, and consider reconstructive visions. That is, if not this, then what? What if all the schools were collapsed, what can be built in their stead, and not just for elites?

Peace,

— *M.*

⊙ ⊙ ⊙

Yo Matt.

I'm going to try and send you something. I don't think I can, however, because it's a dumb question. But you're young and feisty so I'll try. If I can't, you'll know because I won't send anything.

Love,

— *John*

⊙ ⊙ ⊙

Yo John.

All right champ. Great to hear from you as always.

A dumb question? The hell it is. I think it might be *the* question. Deschooling has to be a whole lot more than just

52. Mostly for the endless trash-talk and profanity that we both are known for.

"pull your kids out of school," or else it's just de facto elitism. I don't think it's good enough for us all to be pointing out the insanity of compulsory schools and leaving it there.

There are just way too many kids, way too many families who can't / won't answer that. I'm hardly talking about building another system. We don't need an answer, we need a mass of answers. (I didn't say that, Colin Ward did.) Getting rid of schools, though, has to be a social question, not an atomistic one. Schools have to be replaced / displaced, not just wished away.

How 'bout that?

Peace.

—M.

⊙ ⊙ ⊙

Yo Matt Hern.

OK. A reconstructive vision huh? Yes, that'll be my title. The former Matt Hern, who used to be able to open beer bottles with his teeth, a one-of-a-kind goofy kid, is asking this fat man to be a political visionary, I suppose. Sounds more like Matt Hern PhD, but who am I to knock success?

Without realizing it, you have asked me to substitute one horror, my own reconstructive vision, for the one we have in place. But the problem is in the system, not in its particular character but its systemic nature. It isn't possible to do what Hern asks, no matter how good a system I could invent; in jig time it would corrupt itself into something awful. Open your eyes, the really evil crew are the ones who build the machinery. Call them neo-morlocks. Once coercive power is granted, its continual development into what we now have is absolutely guaranteed.

Here's a test for you: take the ten best public compulsion schools in Canada, make them absolutely voluntary (unlimited absences with no questions asked, no bad record to follow a lad or lassie) and I will bet my bottom dollar that within five years you'll have empty chambers. People don't want to be systematized, even if it's a good system, along with 100 million other units. That isn't how we're built. We voluntarily enter systems and then leave them the same way, but nothing good comes from compulsion. I didn't say that, Plato did.

To grow up correctly we require the absolute right to do the wrong thing from the standpoint of the boss — those who would presume to rule, guide or even cajole humanity into being a mass. All comprehensive systems do that, they can't help themselves, if they aren't systematic they lose their coherence. Liberty is anathema to a reconstructive vision, so fuck it, I'll have none of them.

You need only dip into an almost unbroken, decades-long hum of praise the entire North American intellectual community directed towards the Soviet Union and Mussolini's Italy in the 1920s and '30s to realize how unsuitable any of us are to evaluate and rank the social and political orders of planet Earth — for anyone, that is, other than ourselves and our network of primary associations. We should speak out certainly, but as long as we retain enough humanity to have self-insight not to impose our system on the mind of another. It is far more humane to kill him if his behaviour is intolerable and you get tired of argument.

What we never have the right to do is to trick or coerce others into being pale approximations of ourselves. This is the root cause of genuine Evil that infected this century and the last, an unparalleled century of reconstructive visions. Call it mental colonization, it's worse than death, it makes you a zombie, one of the undead. The truly rotten people do this with a smile on their faces and a lollipop in their hands. They do it for your own good.

Well, fat chance, Dr. Matt, that progress will be made this way, this is the fabled method of positive science transferred to a project to improve the inner life. That's what all schooling is, stripped of its multiple mystiques.

You know something, young scholar, there are many worse fates than ignorance or a short, brutish life — among them having your brain sucked out and your will trampled by people who love you.

Why don't we all understand this? Well, growing up in a culture of secular science which peddles endless novelties as great breakthroughs is part of it; since the young hardly get to see many people struggling hard to find principles and be real, they get confused. People who don't believe in God have a terrible time trying to comprehend what the big deal about Liberty is. I mean, they say, who cares? I've got my car, my split level in the burbs, my telly, my music, my beer — what's all this shit about Liberty? What would I do with it if I did have it, except what I'm doing now?

One way to look at Liberty is that it gives you the right to be free of other people's reconstructive visions so you can search for God's. Of course allowing too many the liberty to do that is fatal to reconstructive visions. And what complicates the picture is that rational people just go nuts trying to understand why — whether it's the Taliban or trailer trash — life struggles against submission to the Scientific Outlook, even though rule by experts would make us healthier, longer-lived, better-fed, in possession of all our teeth and with an urge to get laid even at 100.

That's all true. But the reason to be alive would be gone. Why would you want to live another day, to see another movie? To eat another health salad? To practise another 12-step program for self-improvement?

You say that everywhere you go and lecture, audiences invariably want to ask this sort of question. They say to you, "Matt, give us a significantly articulate reconstructive vision or we refund your fee." So they do that to me too.

And the reason they do is that you and I have conspired to deprive them of their own imaginations and fighting spirits so they fail to realize that their problem really lies in constantly asking experts for solutions.

All experts can do is give you data, information. When they begin to supply you with Wisdom, look out. Let's give the readers of your book a break, Matt, and tell them the truth — the road to Hell lies in trying to organize and rationalize everything, assigning significant decisions to experts. Hidden behind that reasonable social vision of safe, sensible, prosperous reality is the cost of riding that particular gravy train. The ticket price is the right to produce your own life, direct your own time. When you and I produce other people's answers, Matt, we're no better than the folks we attack. Our job is to make the problem easier and clearer to see, maybe to point out a few ways others have tackled the challenge, but always to return to the need for personal struggle.

There is no easy way. No school I've ever seen, even the best of them, ever deals with these vital characteristics of human destiny: that lives most often end in tragedy, that extending life when you have a sensation-centred existence is an act of madness because the stupidity at your core will give you no rest, that failure is a common part of the human condition, that worthwhile pursuits are almost always lonely, that you can neither buy nor negotiate love for yourself, that you can't eat gold, that happiness is absolutely free, and that even the most honourable quests don't always work. And that none of this matters when you own your own spirit. Paradise is writing your own map. If all schools were chained tomorrow, what should the collective "we" do for the collective human race?

Nothing.

Love,

—*John*

⊙ ⊙ ⊙

Yo JTG.

A charming letter as always, my friend. Beautiful one might even call it, but let's have it on.

Let me start this way: a couple of summers ago I was in Sacramento, mouthing off at a homeschoolers' conference, and a woman came up to me after one of my sessions to let me know that she liked what I had to say. She went on to tell me that she had recently pulled her daughter out of school and was very happy with the "results." Mostly, the woman said, it was because her kid was no longer being "brought down" by all the poor, underliterate, underparented and underprivileged children that were in her classes. She continued (not even lowering her voice) to say that the local school system was so untenable because of all the Mexican immigrant kids "flooding" the schools, and she was very relieved to get her child out of that atmosphere.

I'm not making this up, and I think this is important, and not just a wacked Californian. The best critiques of unschooling point to it as just another yuppie middle-class option, another possible "choice" for the most privileged people in world history. Is that all this is? Protecting the rights of those with excess time, money, energy and a penchant for neurotically micromanaging their kids' lives?

Liberty has to exist in something, and right now choice means Coke or Pepsi? Mickey D's or BK? That's about how far market forces have gotten us so far. Charging from the nightmare of compulsorized state schooling into the arms of free-market liberty is not to move very far. Liberty only becomes freedom when it exists in a social milieu; to be free you have to be free from something, and with something else. There are plenty of fates worse than a short, brutish life, especially if it isn't yours.

Which is not the same thing as talking about mass answers at all. Among the most pernicious and central features of the schooled mind is a reliance on experts and professionals for advice and guidance everywhere, not just about how to fix the fan belt and plant zucchinis, but how to get along with your grandma and find peace when she's gone. It's the world of endless management, grief counsellors, self-esteem building, personal excellence, curriculum review panels, self-help, teachers who think they're the reason their students know anything, hordes of bored, mean kids and people who shop when they're lonely. It ain't far from the road to hell, I agree.

Facing that, though, doesn't mean bailing and giving it an

"everyone for themselves" holler on the way out. It is appealing advice in some ways, but it doesn't help much, except letting those who are already doing well off the hook. It might be arguable that humanity resides at the epicentre of biotic evolution, and for better or worse we hold the fate of the planet in our grubby little hands, a reality that makes every caterpillar, manatee, monkey and Douglas fir pretty fucking nervous. Dropping out now and letting the chips fall where they may under the rubric of "liberty" is just running from politics.

People, and the natural world for that matter, will do a whole lot better when spared the constant management and coercion of self-appointed professional for-your-own-gooders. We do need a "mass of answers" though, and we gotta be talking about them, and making them happen, in our neighbourhoods, and not just for ourselves. Reconstruction has to be local, not just individual.

That's the level I want to push this conversation to. I want deschoolers to be talking about *alternatives to school*, that is, social responses to schooling, not just relying on personal or familial answers. You hedge your bets well, talking about a network of primary associations, and I think that's right, as long as that doesn't just mean family, but local community. That's not about describing new systems: local answers are by definition unique and enigmatic and induplicable.

Further, the idea that making schools voluntary would leave them empty is not something I buy. School is not just classes, it is our culture, Illich's global classroom. Make schools voluntary and I bet everyone stays right in place with a little attrition here and there. School control is way past functioning so explicitly, it's an automatic thing, and the student assumes responsibility for the constraints of power; he makes them play spontaneously upon himself; he inscribes in himself the power relation in which he simultaneously plays both roles; he becomes the principle of his own subjection. By this very fact, the external power may throw off its physical weight; it tends to be non-corporeal;

and the more it approaches this limit, the more constant, profound and permanent are its effects: it is a perpetual victory that avoids any confrontation and which is always decided in advance.

I didn't say that, Foucault did.[53] Which is part of why I think homelearners and unschoolers are so important, because there is something so visceral about child-rearing, so instinctual about seeing your kid treated badly, that it can transcend the automatic functioning of a schooled culture, and all those who are committed to its maintenance. But the answers can't be found in the free market, because we're way too far down the path for that. Maybe in a simpler time or place, but not now. The answers have to be found in community.

I mean something very specific there: a place, a comprehensible place that those there recognize and acknowledge. The best definition I have heard is from a Wendell Berry book, relating what an Amish farmer once told him:

> At some point, late in the proceedings, they asked David what community meant to him. He said that when he and his son were plowing in the spring he could look around him and see seventeen teams at work on the neighbouring farms. He knew those teams and the men driving them, and he knew that if he were hurt or sick, those men and those teams would be at work on his farms.[54]

That's really the exact opposite of "everyone for themselves" in some ways, and in some ways not. It is only in community that a living democracy — that is people making real decisions about their lives and resources — can flourish.

"Paradise is writing your own map" is a nice way to put it

53. Michel Foucault, *Discipline and Punish: The Birth of the Prison*, trans. Alan Sheridan (New York: Vintage Books, 1979).
54. Wendell Berry, *Home Economics* (San Francisco: North Point, 1987).

(if a little poetic for my liking, poetry is an insidious vice, and one I note you are susceptible to, a tendency far more dangerous than mine for bourbon), but it has to exist in communities where, to paraphrase WB again, people can trust their liars to be untrustworthy. To ignore that is to invite existing power to rush in: schools brought to you by Wal-Mart. The care of children cannot be left to blocks of entrenched power: not states, nor unions, nor corporations. Resistance can only be about discipline; to ecological ravage, consumerist frenzy and cultural malaise, a discipline that only makes sense as responsibility to the people and the place around you, not just to yourself.

I'm done for now, my friend. I'm sure we'll pick it up again soon. As always, looking forward to the next time we meet. Over and out.

Peace.

—M.

◎ ◎ ◎

Yo Matt Hern.

I received all of your response. Thanks for letting me have the last word. You won't be hearing from me for some time though, as I am currently in full retreat from human contact and hope to enter a vegetative state ere long. Let's leave it at that. Put (c) John Gatto at the bottom of page one.

I hope you remain poor, but this endless stream of writing worries me.

Incidentally, there are no other copies of this essay in existence, so you see how much I trust you, mostly on intuition — I have to be intuitive in your case, because I know that if I got the credit bureau or Interpol on your case my hair would stand on end.

Feel free to change this in any way you like, including putting words and thoughts in my mouth. Remember however, that Lou "Streaky" Gatto, gambling czar of the Genovese family is my cousin and violence is no stranger to me. A word to the wise.

I remain your obedient servant.
John of Pittsburgh

⊙ ⊙ ⊙

Some time after this last letter I send the full text of our con-versation to John for a last perusal. He immediately calls back and fills my machine with three long, bombastic and brilliant messages. Soon after arrives a real last word(s).

⊙ ⊙ ⊙

Dear Matt:

It's 3:25 a.m., I'm seventy years old in ten days (well, sixty-eight). In three hours I'll be at Newark Airport departing for Corpus Christie, from thence to South Padre Island to watch the Sunday football games with an old (older than me) and dear friend. We intend to gamble our brains out, utilizing a bookie in Costa Rica. (If you make a deposit and open an account in my name I'll get some free bets.) I'm betting everything on a six-point two-team teaser which gives me San Francisco even-money over Dallas in Dallas, coupled with Atlanta +10 points over Tampa Bay in Tampa. The spread on San Fran is too low, -41/2 as I write, so I'm suspi-cious. Remember this, young fellow, if it looks too good to be true, it usually isn't true. I've been burned a million times on sure things, but what the hey, we live and we almost never learn. That's the truth.

I have to respond to your wild screed from a failing memory because I can't find it. I did notice, however, how neatly you had me set up for the kill and commend you for having the character that so many of your countrymen lack (Wendy Priesnitz being a big exception) to set up straw men and then mow them down: in that regard you remind me of Michael Moore, the filmmaker. However, unlike Charlton Heston in *Bowling for Columbine*, my own Alzheimer's isn't advanced, so prepare for some incoming from Pittsburgh (sound of American artillery being moved into position).

Now, if memory serves, you want to move me into a box

we might label "Free Market/Hyper-Individualist" while you get to live in the arena of "Loving Community." It's a decent drama, one particularly attractive to the bleeding heart, but at bottom it's a false dichotomy. Real communities are full of cantankerous individuals who put principles (often stupid ones) in front of communitarian blather whenever the mood strikes them. Not always, of course, but often enough that their co-operation can't be taken for granted. See Ken Kesey's *Sometimes a Great Notion* for a look into what I mean. And real individuals (at least the worthy ones) are always heroic defenders of the common good. Joe Campbell has the profile in a book whose title escapes me but which will always be available in college bookstores, forever and ever.

Think of the human race as a work in progress where all formulae are suspect. As long as individuals abound, good communities will be possible, both short- and long-term ones, you can't separate the two things unless you want to parody the little bit of wisdom I've acquired in a long life. Strong people make strong communities, which then extend a hand to the weak, the unfortunate and the young. But musings and speculations arrived at in bull sessions, or by studying Marx and Hegel, that define the ideal community and attempt to legislate it, or otherwise impose it, lead to stagnant suburbs and communes which quickly decay into places unpleasant.

I lived through the great wave of communitarian experimentation of the late '60s, and found myself charmed and beguiled by it like so many others, and watched in horror as every single one of these experiments and every single "open" classroom, corrupted, became doctrinaire, or disbanded. I don't know a single exception. However noble the abstraction, in the execution an aura of childishness descended upon the experiment, a climate of pettiness and contention, antagonisms generated out of (at least nominally) different interpretations of the sacred message.

Am I being sarcastic, cynical, defeatist? God, I hope not. I think my candour stems from having so little time left to hold it precious and hating seeing living energy wasted in tilting at windmills. If you teach children to be self-reliant, self-sufficient, possessed of valuable skills, full of curiosity, physically strong, relentlessly analytical when the situation calls for that, civil, kind, pious, courageous, they will reach, like plants reach for the sun, for good communities.

But if, like Pestalozzi, Froebel and the social-work mind, you tell them this or that is the way we behave in a good community, they will rebel eventually, in thought, deed or both, because they will know you are lying. You should have figured out by now that the only thing you really have to teach kids about life is taught by the way you live it. Schools are a supermarket of human style and kids are excellent judges of human products. The texts, drills, environments and experiences are always secondary — what matters is what you have made of yourself. There is no way to represent the community in your behaviour with "teachings" without having the best kids revolt or hold you in contempt. Be who you want them to be yourself, on the other hand, and chances are good that you can contribute a building block or two to the lives under your stewardship.

For most of modern history, school has had three purposes: 1) to make good people, call that the religious purpose; 2) to make good citizens, call that the public or community purpose; 3) to make individuals their personal best so that they can lead good lives, good individual lives. What stole in to corrupt this equation big-time in the twentieth century was a bizarre Fourth Purpose (that's the title of a film I'm trying to make if you can help me raise the money) to look at kids as raw material, "human resources" for the construction of an efficient economy and governance system. It's a vile, horrible perspective which leads to the compounds of habit-training and attitude adjustment we call institutional schooling.

I know your motives are better than that, but you have to be aware of the similarities between the tyranny we have and tyranny you would impose — if you helped to create non-voluntary, expert-driven structures — so that everyone could enjoy the world as you see it in your opium dreams.

Crudely put, I want a world where if you piss me off too outrageously I can break your nose and feel good about it. And if the government pisses me off through one or another of its agents, and wears out my patience, I can pick up a gun and shoot the tax collector. Remember Robin Hood?

Would that be a perfect world? Hardly. It would be one full of stress and strife and moral choices and responsibility for one's action, a surprising, dynamic, messy, chaotic place. That's what human beings are, school can only deaden this humanity, not alter it for long. I recommend a close reading of three Biblical texts: Job, Proverbs and Ecclesiastes for understanding. Indeed if I had a school program of the sort I think you are groping toward, *I'd make them required reading.*

The best and almost only way to improve schools is to improve yourself. Your assignment is to think about that.

Best love to you Matt.

John Taylor Gatto

◎ ◎ ◎

The conversation continues.

2 Free to Learn

The teacher thought hard for a while. "Suppose instead we all sing a little song," she suggested.

    All the children stood up by their seats except Pippi; she stayed where she was on the floor. "You go ahead and sing," she said. "I'll rest myself a while. Too much learning breaks even the healthiest."

    But now the teacher's patience had come to an end.[55]

Learning Units

Throughout this chapter I am going to look at various aspects of pedagogical thinking and how the political and structural realities of school dominate current discourses about how kids learn. I think it's important to spend a little time considering how kids learn in schools, and what factors influence and direct the way schools educate.

    So often when I speak, people (very often teachers) will complain that my comments are unrealistic, that their everyday reality is kids in classes sitting in rows in front of them and they have to deal with that. I have some genuine sympathy for the work-with-

---

55. Lindgren, *Pippi Longstocking*, 56.

what-we-have point; at the same time, it is indicative of the ass-backwards way we tend to think of learning.

Far too often we demand that individuals, in this case children, adapt themselves to fit institutional needs. I am interested in the reverse line of thinking, that institutions have to be retrofitted to be able to meet the needs and desires of those they are purporting to serve. It is institutional intransigence that so often refuses to acknowledge individual difference and instead turns to more and more baroque and intrusive treatments, from drugs like Ritalin to behaviour modification therapies to administrative techniques that enforce compliance. That conversation begs to be turned on its head.

It is a truism that people learn best when they are following their own interests, passions and motivations. It is not a complicated or particularly controversial idea, at least in everyday, non-academic conversation, although it is ignored as a matter of course. The reverse is equally true in that it is very difficult for people to learn, to be instructed, to take in information when they are not interested or motivated. This is immediately obvious to anyone who has worked with kids or tried to teach anything, at any level. People who don't want to be in your class, who are there for reasons other than their own or who would rather leave are difficult to engage, and they have little real interest in the material. People who are eager and have their own reasons and motivations for learning are often difficult to hold back.

This underlies so much of what is immediately and evidently wrong with schools. Teachers are coping with curricular materials that they had no part in creating, may or may not have any genuine interest in, and may or may not have any knowledge of. Teachers are essentially being asked to act as a conduit, passing on information from above on down below. There are many more sub-aspects of their jobs, and most teachers are able to do fine work within narrow confines, but pedagogically speaking it is a next-to-impossible place to work from.

Students, on the other hand, are being asked to sit in classrooms with thirty other kids of the same age, for five to six hours a day, five days a week, ten months a year, for a minimum of twelve years. They are listening to a teacher they may or may not know at all, telling them about subjects they had no part in choosing, that they may or may not care about at all. It is hardly fertile ground to work with, and yet that is the school baseline. Teachers are being asked to spin gold out of straw.

Imagine for a moment that someone calls up and asks you if you'd mind watching thirty kids at your house tomorrow. You will be paid relatively well, but there are a few requirements. Not only do you have to deal with thirty kids, you have to keep them largely confined to one room. You will have some limited resources at your disposal, some books, some games, some gadgets, but you have to stay inside for the bulk of the day. As well, the children are expected to be orderly, polite, quiet and docile. You are welcomed to use any bribe or threat you can legally conceive of to ensure this. Further, you will be given a book of varying (and unrelated) subject matter that you will be expected to learn yourself and transmit to all the kids. They will be tested at the end of the day, and both you and they will be evaluated based on the results.

This sounds like a job that no right-minded person would take. Yet it is one that millions upon millions of students and teachers across Canada and the U.S. take as a given every day. The business of schools is an absurd proposition and one that cannot possibly meet expectations without a complex and punitive system of control, massive social pressures, extreme institutional technique, constant media campaigns and deeply committed state compulsion.

⊙ ⊙ ⊙

This is the foundation that schools have to build on, and from which they begin to develop educational approaches. Schools are pedagogically driven by the need to keep children engaged and off the street while their parents go to work, while more generalized

goals around education and preparing children for the workforce
have to adapt to this exigency. Many people have commented to
me, "Without schools the economy would collapse. People could-
n't go to work." This is exactly right, but it is more accurate to say
that the way we construct schools is fundamental to the way we
construct economic life.

Schools are designed to cope with as many kids as possible, for
as long as possible, for as cheaply as possible, and those limits are
constantly being pushed (see preschools, after-school care, constant budgetary scrapping, etcetera). Considerations of how kids
can learn, develop and thrive must coincide with this reality or
they are not of much use to school people. The basic structure of
schools dominates and profoundly limits discussions of what it
might mean for kids to grow up right and learn well. Unless the
conversation is reversed and it becomes a question of what conditions kids around us need to thrive, pedagogical discussions are
extremely limited.

Even in many pleasant, small and progressive schools that I
have visited across the continent, teachers always speak of the
strain of keeping students attending. Compelling kids to come all
day, every day to classes they are fundamentally disinterested in is
a struggle, even for decent and humane school people. There is
nothing quite so discouraging as standing in front of a group of
people who would leave if you gave them even half a chance. It is a
truly lousy feeling that almost all of us have experienced at one
time or another. It is the constant struggle that so many of us
remember from our own school days, battling the "for your own
good" mantra, and which is in part responsible for intense
burnout / dropout rates among teachers as well as students.

Kids and teachers across North America drop out at a rate that
is far greater than is often officially acknowledged, with much
higher rates in very poor areas, aboriginal communities and minority neighbourhoods. The baseline for British Columbia, for example, according to ministry spokespeople, is that 25 percent of stu-

dents entering into Grade 8 do not finish within six years. Add to that smaller attrition rates for younger grades, and the oft-repeated figure of 30 percent is accurate. Regarding teacher attrition rates, "the U.S. Department of Education predicts that American schools will need two million new teachers over the next decade. As daunting as that task seems, it gets more so when you consider that 20 to 50 percent of these new teachers will quit within the first five years."[56]

In British Columbia, 20 percent of teachers leave the profession within their first four years, and that is among the lowest figures on the continent. There is currently a worldwide shortage of teachers that is becoming desperate in many parts of North America, due in part to retirement, expanding student populations and teachers quitting early. In parts of the U.S. there are major teacher inducement and recruitment schemes underway, including signing bonuses — sometimes as large as twenty grand, as in Massachusetts, for example.

Given these sizable impediments to success and the scale of the job they are being asked to perform, it is hardly surprising that schools have developed such intricate systems of teaching technique, bribe / threat inducement, surveillance, monitoring, discipline and punishment, reward, testing, evaluation and compulsion. Michel Foucault's analysis of Bentham's panopticon has been overused, but his descriptions of external and internal authoritarian control remain useful in considering schools. Even the worst schools are not prisons, but operate on the same (muted) logic of containment and correction.

Foucault, in speaking of Jeremy Bentham's prison model, described a circular prison in which all the cells face in towards a courtyard in which there is a single guard tower. The cells are back-

56. Amy C. Colley, "What Can Principals Do About New Teacher Attrition?" *Principal Magazine* 81, no. 4 (March 2002) <www.naesp.org/comm/po302b.htm>.

lit so all the prisoners are always visible to the guards, but the guards are always invisible. The prison becomes a "machine for creating and sustaining a power relation independent of the person who exercises it; in short, that the inmates should be caught up in a power situation of which they themselves are the bearers."[57]

Since the prisoners never know when the guards are watching them specifically, they have to assume they are always being watched. Then the guards can slowly be reduced from many to one — even to none — and still the prisoners never know who or what is guarding them. In time, even the bars can be removed as confinement becomes a state of mind, and the inmates will eventually imprison themselves.

Foucault had specific social implications in mind, and many others have adapted his ideas, but it is not much of a jump to think of schooling. Kids are watched, guarded, drug-tested, drug-dog sniffed, metal-detected, scanned and monitored so consistently in schools that in short time they begin to do the job themselves, internalizing compulsion and convincing themselves that it is the curriculum that knows what and when they should be learning, not themselves.

Once that process has taken place, kids become strangers to self-motivation, self-discipline and the argument reinforces itself: "See? These kids don't have any interest in learning, they don't want to read, they don't have active minds. If we don't force them to come here, if we don't force them to engage with knowledge they will grow up ignorant and incapable of participating in the wider culture, let alone getting a job." The pieces fit, and kids and families buy the argument that unless they are coerced to learn they won't thrive.

The kids that I know (and I dare say all kids) do not want to grow up stupid, ignorant, lazy or illiterate. No one does. Everyone wants to be knowledgable, competent, confident, articulate and

57. Foucault, *Discipline and Punish* (New York: Vintage), 200.

literate. There are many things that can impede that outcome, perhaps the most prominent of which is schooling. There is nothing like compulsion, arbitrary authority and forced learning to sour people's enthusiasms, natural curiosity and trust in themselves. There is nothing like the teaching of reading or math to kill a child's desire to read and work well with numbers.

◎ ◎ ◎

Radical critiques of school pedagogy have tended to thread around the argument that state schools are designed by dominant social interests and will necessarily support them. I believe that there are elements of truth to the idea that schools are primarily about citizen production, and in a particularly postmodern way I think those dynamics have become largely subsumed. Contemporary pedagogy has emerged in response to institutional imperatives: that is to say that how kids are taught and dealt with primarily emerges not from larger ideals about citizenry, but from very immediate and everyday management needs.

More than ever before, the way we speak of learning and education is driven by the discourses of management and organizational theory. Given class size, seat-hours, grade-point expectations, instruction hours and money spent, how is that we can design the most efficient and useful system? What techniques are most useful in dealing with the clients / units and moving them through the system? What are the tools that can allow for maximum potentiality to be realized?

Politically and culturally, ideals about citizenry may still hold some resonance, but pedagogically the school questions are all bureaucratic and systematic. Larger, more complexly ambiguous concerns come a distant second, if and when there is time and energy to consider them.

Teaching versus Learning

If contemporary ideas about pedagogy have emerged overwhelmingly from bureaucratic and functional school realities, what can we make of the practice of teaching?

I was riding a train a couple of years ago, on my way from Montreal to lecture at a small university in the Maritimes. It was a long trip and I spent most of it in the company of two older women who were coming back from a weekend of gambling in Quebec. They were former schoolteachers, happily retired. When they found out that I was off to give a course called the "Philosophy of Education," they were very interested in what I was planning to say. They asked questions and listened for a while, and finally one of them interrupted me and said, "Listen, honey, I've taught thousands of kids. Thousands of kids. Seen 'em all. And in the end there's just one thing you need to know: sometimes you can't pour a gallon into a cup. That's it." I thanked her kindly and we moved our discussion on.

I really liked those women and enjoyed their company, and that conversation has stayed with me for a lot of reasons. I think it is a very accurate assessment of how we view teaching: kind of as a shipping / receiving thing, taking information / knowledge / skills from one place and transferring them to another.

The contemporary act of teaching is largely technique that has been disembedded from its original roots in mentoring, modelling and skill / knowledge-based instruction. The line goes: *If you can't do, teach*. We all know of teachers who are in their occupation because their original ideas about what they were going to do with their lives failed to pan out. It is a cliché that teaching is the ubiquitous fallback position.

There is a great section from Vinoba Bhave's book *The Intimate and the Ultimate* that I like to read out often. It is longish, but I think it makes the point sweetly. Bhave founded the Bhoodan Yajna, or land-gift movement, in India in 1951, walking across the country, gathering donations of more than five million acres of land and redistributing it to the poor. Gandhi identified Bhave as his spiritual successor.

> A young man said that he wished to do some good work for society.
>
> "Tell me," I said, "what kind of work do you feel you could do well?"
>
> "Only teaching, I think," replied the young man. "I can't do anything else, I can only teach, but I am interested in it and feel sure that I shall be able to do it well."
>
> "Yes, yes, I do not doubt that, but what are you going to teach? Spinning? Carding? Weaving? Could you teach any of these?"
>
> "No, I can't teach those."
>
> "Then tailoring, or dyeing, or carpentry?"
>
> "No, I know nothing about them."
>
> "Perhaps you could teach cooking, grinding, and other household skills?"
>
> "No, I have never done any work like that. I can only teach . . ."
>
> "My dear friend, you answer 'No' to every question, and yet you keep saying you can only teach. What do you mean? Can you teach gardening?"
>
> The would-be teacher said, rather angrily, "Why do you ask all this? I told you at the beginning, I can do nothing else. I can teach literature."
>
> "Good! Good! I am beginning to understand now. You mean you can teach people to write books like Tagore and Shakespeare?"
>
> This made the young man so angry that he began to splutter.
>
> "Take it easy," I laughed. "Can you teach patience?"
>
> That was too much.[58]

58. Vinoba Bhave, *The Intimate and the Ultimate* (London: Harper Collins, 1991), quoted in Matt Hern, ed., *Deschooling Our Lives* (Gabriola Island, B.C.: New Society, 1996), 19-20.

I don't want to wax rhapsodic about manual labour particularly, though there is something very important there, but I think Bhave's portrayal of teaching rationales makes sense in light of schooling's institutional needs: teachers need to know how to manage groups of kids primarily, and skill or knowledge are secondary. Contemporary teachers are not required to have any basic skills to pass on, let alone any real capacity in the subjects they teach, aside from knowledge of the curriculum.

Elsewhere in *The Intimate and the Ultimate*, Bhave speaks to part of what I am really after here: the tenuous relationship between teaching and learning and the dubiousness of teaching itself.

> An interesting light is cast on the Indian attitude to education by the fact that in all fourteen languages of India there is no root word corresponding to English "teach." In these languages we can learn, we can help others to learn, but we cannot teach. The use of the two distinct words, "teach" and "learn," suggests that these two processes may be thought of as independent from one another. But that is merely the professional vanity of the "teacher," and we shall not understand the nature of education unless we rid ourselves of that vanity.[59]

It is not that I believe it is impossible for one person to pass on information or skill to another. It is that I see teachers and teaching taking illegitimate credit for the development of the people around them. After years and years of working with children intensively, I remain thoroughly unconvinced that there is such a thing as "teaching" and that if there is, its relationship to learning, if *that* can be said to be a "thing," is very questionable.

⊘ ⊘ ⊘

59. *Ibid.*, 18.

I tend to think that neither teaching nor learning are actual processes or events so much as they are value judgments. Part of what is at stake here is the *control* of what we call learning: where it happens, how it happens, under what conditions and for what ends.

In a lot of ways learning is synonymous with living. Learning is something that happens all the time, whether we intend it or not. Learning is what people do. We learn, take in new information, gain new knowledge, pick up new skills and insights constantly. Even if you were locked in an iron box and buried in the ground you would learn all kinds of things, not least of which would be what it is like to be buried in a locked iron box. People learn in all kinds of constantly shifting ways, and while we certainly develop when we can direct that learning in purposeful and considered ways, it is hardly an exclusive route to growth, intellectual or otherwise.

Largely I think the word learning signifies control. It identifies an activity that the designator approves of: Now you're learning something ... I hope you learned your lesson ... When will you ever learn? It points to an activity that is judged useful, valuable or appropriate, or at least classifiable. It is how teachers and school people can distinguish between activities that are designed, planned and monitored for "your own good," and other non-official ones. It is the difference between a simplistic elementary classroom math exercise that is called "learning" and kids talking about hockey statistics and adding point totals and dividing games played by goals scored that is called something else (usually wasting time).

There is absolutely no question that people, young and old, can acquire all kinds of complex skills and knowledges without being taught. The examples are all around us and have been exhaustively documented.[60] Almost all children, for example, learn to talk at an

---

60. Maybe my favourite books on learning without teaching are John Holt's *Learning All the Time* (Reading, Mass.: Addison-Wesley, 1989) and *Never Too Late: My Musical Life Story* (New York: Delacorte Press, 1978).

incredibly early age. How is it that we trust kids to pick up insanely complicated languages like English between the ages of one and three with an absolute minimum of instruction, and yet a few years later presume that they need constant "teaching" to learn how to read? Children absolutely do not need to be taught how to read. In fact, the practice of teaching it is the biggest impediment there is to children becoming confident, eager, capable readers.

As Grace Llewellyn says, the desire to learn and thrive and develop is inherent to us. Social circumstances, school not the least of them, compel so many to bury their best and most eager impulses.

> If you had always been free to learn, you would follow your natural tendency to find out as fully as possible about the things that interest you, cars or stars. We are all born with what they call "the love of learning," but it dives off into an elusive void when we go to school.[61]

In a thoroughly schooled culture, though, this line of thinking seems absurd to many. Lots of people I know really believe that no one can learn without being taught and that unless they are driven by the external motivations of compulsory schooling they will intellectually decompose. They believe they have to rely on institutions to develop knowledge or skills, and in some ways this is true — a reality that will only recede as the dominance of schooling wanes.

Anyone who spends any time at all with kids can cite experiences they have had with children learning complex things on their own. I know a kid who learned how to read when he was five, sitting in the back of the car; he was so bored on the long ride that he

61. Grace Llewellyn, *The Teenage Liberation Handbook: How to Quit School and Get a Real Life and Education* (Eugene, Ore.: Lowry House, 1991), 43.

figured out how to read with a bird identification book. I have no idea how my oldest daughter, now eleven, learned to read. She was, and still is, read to all the time and has always loved books. She spent many hours looking through picture books on her own. One day when she was six I noticed that she was staring at a volume from the Narnia series for a very long time, and a brief check confirmed that she did in fact know what the words were saying. I have asked, but really neither she nor I have much idea how it happened. Certainly no one taught her. Maybe she wanted it so badly that she willed reading to happen. Maybe she memorized a short book and went from there. Who knows? And really, I don't think it matters much, except to professional educators who want to treat children as part of a larger technical problem to be solved and systematized.

The real issue is that the act of learning has become thoroughly attached to the idea of teaching. Once learning has been disembedded from its place in everyday life, it becomes the province of institutions and professionals, and people become less and less able to view learning as theirs, to recognize that their own flourishing is their own responsibility.

As John Holt says, "The most important thing any teacher has to learn, not to be learned in any school of education I ever heard of, can be expressed in seven words: *learning is not the product of teaching*. Learning is the product of the activity of learners."[62]

Teaching is now widely believed to be a prerequisite for learning, whether in schools or out. At the heart of why this is so important is the rise of disabling professions like teaching. When a culture becomes accustomed to the idea that learning relies on teaching, people become reliant on authority, less capable as individuals and more willing to await direction before action. It is the pedagogical premise that enables centralization of authority,

---

62. John Holt, *Growing Without Schooling*, quoted in Llewellyn, *The Teenage Liberation Handbook*, 53.

power and control at a wider political level. When people believe that other authorities — experts and professionals — are best able to make fundamental decisions about their learning and health, it is not surprising that they come to feel the same way about political decisions.

◎ ◎ ◎

Brazilian popular education theorist, writer and activist Paulo Freire describes prevailing pedagogy as "the banking concept of education":

> Education is suffering from narration sickness . . . Narration (with the teacher as narrator) leads students to memorize mechanically the narrated content. Worse yet, it turns them into "containers" or "receptacles" to be "filled" by the teacher. The more completely she fills the receptacles, the better a teacher she is. The more meekly the receptacles allow themselves to be filled, the better students they are.
>
>   Education thus becomes an act of depositing, in which the students are depositories and the teacher is the depositor. Instead of communicating, the teacher issues communiqués and makes deposits which the students patiently receive, memorize and repeat. This is the "banking" concept of education . . . with the ideological intent (often not perceived by educators) of indoctrinating them to adapt to the world of oppression.[63]

It isn't much of a stretch to describe this as a very regular, widely accepted definition of teaching and learning. In answer, Freire counterposes a problem-posing, liberating praxis that engages teachers and students in dialogical relations, "posing the problems of human beings in their relations with the world."[64]

63. Paulo Freire, *The Paulo Freire Reader*, eds. Ana Maria Araujo Freire and Donaldo Macedo (New York: Continuum, 1998), 67.
64. *Ibid.*, 74.

Occasionally I encounter people speaking of these pedagogical distinctions as somehow frivolous side issues to real radical social transformation, but as Freire emphasizes repeatedly, liberation is a praxis, and the banking method, or compulsorized schooling, lays the essential groundwork for a culture and society based on domination. The actual curriculum that is being transmitted by schools includes, but is not limited to, these ideas: *follow orders, know your place, allow others to decide what you need to learn, democracy is only relative, culture is official.* A liberatory pedagogical praxis is at the heart of liberatory change.

That praxis has to be based in relationships within and developing from community and the local control of the resources that are now being absorbed by schools. What Freire calls a problem-posing education has to be a locally rooted activity because the conditions in which learning occurs are essential to its character.

$$\circledcirc \quad \circledcirc \quad \circledcirc$$

Reconceiving teaching and learning has to include all kinds of currently neglected styles that were once relied upon for the acquisition of skill and knowledge: mentorships, modelling, internships, practice, private experimentation, training and so much else. It must rest on the idea that people understand best how they themselves learn. To paraphrase John Taylor Gatto, there is no body of knowledge that accurately describes how kids learn. Learning is so enigmatic and dependent on circumstance and personality that I have trouble understanding how I learn, let alone my daughters, let alone groups of kids and let alone *all* children. I am deeply suspicious of anyone or anything — from self-styled gurus like Maria Montessori, Jean Piaget and Rudolf Steiner, to curriculum guides, to the wall of conferencing / workshopping "learning experts" — claiming to have "discovered" methodologies for teaching. I think it largely fantasy, a suspicion that is reinforced for me every time I hang out with kids. What we call "learning" is so complex, so fluid and so dependent on relationship that it defies the easy categorizations school people are so desperate to find.

In many ways, I think that the only thing you can teach is yourself. I think it essentially true that a person can only guide or drive his or her own learning. Taken differently, I think it also true that what we call "good teachers" are people who are able to convey a sense of themselves, who can reveal, make transparent and accessible, their own understanding and analysis. I consider it entrenched vanity that many teachers believe they can transmit or bank information better than others, that their technique is transferable, that they are able to teach almost anyone because they have mastered methodologies that "work." Too many teachers think they can pour faster, more efficiently and without spilling too much. It is the professionalization of one of the most basic and fundamental pieces of everyday life and the suppression of personality in favour of technique.

Why do we call reading a book and retaining the information "teaching yourself," but listening to someone convey the same information verbally "being taught"? Is going to a lecture being taught? What about watching a video of the same lecture? I think the fundamental difference is engagement, and what we think of as "good teaching" is the ability to allow others into your world, to view your understanding of the subject, to engage and dialogue with it. At root, the issue is one of relationship, context and intent: the difference between shaping people and people designing / driving themselves.

It is admittedly difficult to speak of these things because the words have become so systematically conflated and malleable. I think it important in some ways not to become ideological, and the terms themselves are only important in what they point to specifically. I think there is reason to doubt and question both the use of and ideas behind *teaching* and *learning*. They now point largely to officially acceptable activities, not to the universally understood acts of growing and thriving. I think it is evident that only locally constructed relationships, control and direction can determine the quality and nature of learning experiences, and that self-direction is fundamental to the learning people consider integral to the good life.

The Nature of Authority

Recently I was at Windsor House, a North Vancouver free school I have been part of for a long time, sitting outside near the playground. It was a bright sunny day and there were kids all over, running through the forest, playing on the equipment, picking blackberries. Near me there was a huge pile of blackberry branches, maybe four feet high and five feet across. On top of the pile was a layer of grass clippings, covering the branches like icing on a cake.

As I was sitting there, basking in the sun, a small boy came running by on a raised level of the playground somewhat above me. I didn't recognize him, nor he me, as it was early in the year and it was one of his first days there. He looked down at the huge pile beside me, and from his perspective it was an enormous, soft pile of grass — a big pillow waiting to be leapt on. I sensed immediately what he was planning and realized that he couldn't see the pile was actually a cunning (if unintended) trap.

Realizing disaster was imminent, I put my hand out and told him to stop. He looked puzzled, so I said, "Hey buddy, I know that pile looks terrific to jump into, but it's actually full of brambles. You're going to be bummed if you dive in there." It was evident right away that he had no interest in listening to me. I tried again quickly, "I wouldn't do that pal. Seriously. That pile is *full* of blackberry branches!" No luck.

The kid had one last glance at me and jumped the three feet down to the pile. It was a disaster, albeit a minor one. He was immediately up to his neck in blackberry brambles, all scratched up and dismayed. He was screaming and crying as his father and I pulled him out, legs and arms flailing and bloodied. He was also furious at me, for what I am not exactly sure, but there was no mistaking that.

The kid had every reason and no reason at all to trust me. I was just a random adult sitting there, and in one sense he might have guessed that I had some valuable information for him. From another perspective, though, I was just another adult trying to get in the way of his good time. To my mind, he made the wrong choice. I was offering a voice of authority that had some real basis and natural weight: I could see what he couldn't. He, however, assumed that I was just trying to stop him from jumping for some bureaucratic, teacher-like, mean-spirited reason: manipulative authority. I was attempting to help him out, and he guessed that I was pushing him around randomly. Unfortunately, he guessed wrong.

John Holt, George Dennison,[65] Grace Llewellyn[66] and many others have written about the differences between manipulative and natural authority, and frankly I can't add much to their insights. I do want to make a small point though: in a time of increasing authoritarianism, I think it is critically important for kids to be able to see and feel and smell different layers and kinds of authority. There is little question that we are witnessing and experiencing levels of official authority the likes of which we have never before seen in this part of the world, and learning how to respond will be crucial to our future.

We are surrounded by institutional authority, and its pervasive-

65. George Dennison, *The Lives of Children*, quoted in John Holt, *Instead of Education* (New York: Dutton, 1976), explains the "important distinction between natural authority, which rests on experience, competence, wisdom and commitment and the respect, trust and love of one person for another, and official or coercive authority, which rests only on the power to bribe, threaten and punish. Many people find it hard to understand this difference, or to see that coercive authority does not complement and support natural authority, but undermines and destroys it."
66. Llewellyn, *The Teenage Liberation Handbook*: "One of the worst things about this sort of arbitrary authority is that it makes us lose our trust of natural authority — people who know what they're doing and could share a lot of wisdom with us."

ness is part of who we are: from security guards to teachers to police officers to immigration officials. While each person or relationship contains various layers of authority, of all different kinds, distinguishing between them is an important skill to nurture. I am not talking about some kind of extrasensory perception, but a quality that only time, experience and mistakes can develop.

One of the key aspects of schooling is that it allows very little chance for kids to learn how to negotiate those differences: authority is virtually all coercive in schools, all the way around; administrators, teachers and students are all being pushed around by manufactured rationales that are not their own. In my example of the brambles, the young lad didn't even consider that my suggestions might be well-meaning and legitimately heartfelt. It is only in moving through the culture that kids can begin to build up the reservoir of direct experience that they need to draw on for making delineations, decisions and useful choices. When kids are removed from the broader culture and isolated in schools, all authority becomes blurred, the world *in toto* manipulative, and crude self-interest perhaps the most comfortable place of retreat.

John Taylor Gatto has said over and over that we have to learn how to author our own stories, and in some ways that is exactly right. In other ways it obscures some truth because we are not walking alone; we need to rely on the guidance, advice, mentorship, friendship and care of many others. We all need to be able to develop bonds of trust and learn to identify who we can rely on, who can support our own autonomy and not subject us to official or manipulative decision-making. To flourish we must be able to find parts of the culture that are not coercive, find natural authority to trust and distinguish between them. That process should really be started as soon as possible, so kids can have the opportunity to make mistakes, find their way and author themselves.

☉ ☉ ☉

Deschooling is often misrepresented as leaving kids alone, a kind of do-it-yourself ethic gone wild, but it is never like that. We all live in complex social webs, and even (or especially) the youngest of kids have to make decisions about their time based on what everyone else around them is doing. The thrust of unschooling is giving kids as much control, or authority, as possible, and not just over their "educational" choices, but over all the decisions that a full life entails. Those decisions can never be made in anything resembling isolation; they are full of complexity. What and how you want to learn is something a lot more than choosing Coke or Pepsi.

It is not that kids should be left to make every decision about what to do with their time; it is about actively living from a place of engagement. So many times people have asked me, "How is an eight-year-old going to know what she wants to be when she grows up? How can she know what she should be learning?" The implication is that adult professionals need to decide for kids what should and should not be known and how it should be approached.

I think that question should be turned around. How is an eighteen-year-old who has never been allowed to make decisions about her life going to know how to organize her days after spending the last thirteen years of her life answering the bell, reading what she is told to, sitting in a class and following the most prescribed of programs? That to me is a much more pressing query. Our kids spend their entire natural youths developing virtually no decision-making capacity. They rarely have a chance to pursue genuinely independent study, and every day is organized for them into randomly associated fragments while their ethical judgments are reduced to what is and isn't allowed. And *then*, after thirteen years of that, they are turned out and expected to know how to make good decisions about their lives — and critical decisions at that. Everything is dropped in front of high-school graduates with the expectation that they are ready, and yet they've had amazingly limited experience with living in a complex world.

I don't want to suggest that there are only two kinds of authority, natural or manipulative. That easy distinction is far too simplistic, and one that deschoolers are often too quick to jump on.
Neither people nor institutions can be described so flatly. In every
circumstance there are infinitely variegated and confused layers of
control. There are endless Foucauldian[67] power dynamics in any
relationship, it is not about ignoring or trying to destroy authority.
Authority can never be expunged, it is present always, but it has to
be about acknowledging where authority sits and being able to
answer it. The act of negotiating authority is infinitely complicated
and complicating and can be partially described as "learning how
to make one's way in the world," which has to be much more than
simply learning how to do what you are told.

Despite many a liberal teacher's best attempts, the imperative of
curriculum-driven agendas renders authority simplistic and largely
one-dimensional. The relationships between administrators and
teachers, teachers and students, and teachers and parents are carefully constructed and maintained by prescribed power relationships.
Everyone has a very clear idea where they sit in the institutional
structure before entering in. There is constant movement and gra-
dation, but the schooled curriculum resists complexity at every step.

The institution of school is so widely understood that its maintenance is mostly a matter of culture. Teachers teach what they are
told to teach, students listen, absorb what they can and then repeat
it. That's school. It is largely fruitless for a student (or teacher) to
attempt to use school as a vehicle for genuine inquiry for all kinds
of specific and obvious reasons. That is simply not what it is about
and everyone knows it.

67. For his analyses of power, see Michel Foucault, *The History of Sexuality* ,
Vol. 1: An Introduction (New York: Pantheon, 1978), *Power / Knowledge*
(New York: Pantheon, 1980), *Discipline and Punish* (New York: Pantheon,
1977), *Madness and Civilization* (New York: Vintage Books, 1973) and/or
Foucault Live (Interviews, 1966–84). (New York: Semiotext(e): 1989).

The nature of school authority is that students and teachers are completely replaceable at any single point. One teacher leaves and another replaces her and no one misses a step. One student moves on, another takes his place and the structure remains intact. Schools are designed specifically so that authority does not rest with any individual lest the entire structure become unstable. At every point, real authority is invested in the position, not the person. This is very key to the success of schools.

It is in this that people know, almost instinctively, how to act in schools. There are roles kids can fill (for example, class clown, troublemaker, suck, quiet one), but these are much less than real personalities. Students, teachers and administrators alike have a limited set of choices and roles they can fill, and it is understood that everyone is replaceable. Interestingly, real authority in a school lies with no one.

◉ ◉ ◉

Kids face a complex and layered world, one with bewildering levels and combinations of authority. To be able to act in the world, to be able to swim instead of being washed away, they have to have had real experience. It is certainly true that heavily schooled children are often eminently capable of negotiating huge bureaucracies, and this really is a useful skill. Unfortunately, bureaucracies are the only kind of social structures schooled kids have had experience with, so they tend to seek them out and replicate them. To be part of a community, to actively participate in the world, kids need to experience moving in the larger world from a very young age.

The drive to act, not just be acted upon, runs into institutional renditions of authority. Moving with confidence in the world requires experience and the capacity to test authority, learn about responding to failure and put success in perspective. It is the kind of messiness and irreplaceable, unreplicable activity that simply cannot be reduced into curriculum. All of it requires the experience of negotiating the larger community and practising the practice of authority.

The Value of Play

Throughout radical pedagogical thinking, maybe most prominently in free-schooling and deschooling literatures, run some very serious beliefs about the value of play. These beliefs have filtered into mainstream liberal school ideas as well, influencing child-centred approaches and inculcating themselves into curricula, especially for younger kids. While I think much of this discourse is pointed in the right direction, I also think that easy platitudes about the goodness of play mask some deeper cultural issues.

Listen to what Mimsy Sadofsky has to say in describing what students do at the Sudbury Valley School, one of the oldest and most successful non-coercive schools in the U.S.:

> Doing what they choose to do is the common theme; learning is the by-product. It is first and foremost a place where students are free to do what we all do when we have the time to, and what we all find to be the most satisfactory — they play.
>
> Play is the most serious pursuit at Sudbury Valley. This is not an accident. Psychologists pretty much agree these days that allowing the mind to roam freely has the most potential for mind expansion. In fact, when we talk about our most creative moments, we describe them as "playing with new ideas" . . .
>
> Children who play constantly do not draw an artificial line between work and play. In fact, you could say that they are working constantly if you did not see the joy in the place, a joy most usually identified with the pursuit of avocations.[68]

68. Mimsy Sadofsky, "A School for Today," in *Deschooling Our Lives*, ed. Hern, 121-122.

I like a lot of this, yet find much in it to dispute. The places I have put my heart into over the last decade or so can certainly be described in terms of play. Chris Mercogliano, director of the Albany Free School (one of my favourite places), says that the AFS looks like a Montessori school "after a high wind came through." I have heard people say that the places I run look like schools at recess. I want my daughters to play as much as possible for as long as possible. At the same time, I do not hold *play* to be the essential description of thriving activity.

Play is most often counterposed with *work*, which is itself often conflated with *employment*. To a large extent, play is described as fun, leisure and triviality. Work is toil, labour and usefulness. Play is often held as important only in that it relaxes and readies one for work. Articulations of liberatory pedagogical praxis often want to turn this around, especially for children, and describe play as important in and of itself. This line of thinking has an Aristotelian origin, in that he described leisure as when people could express themselves most fully. Aristotle (among many prominent others since) believed that it was in times of leisure that people had the opportunity to become themselves, to find space for creative endeavours that developed their potentialities most fully.[69]

I have long had argument with this stance because in my heart I believe something like the opposite. I think it is in times of work that people are the best of themselves. All toil is noble in some senses, though I am in no way referring to employment here because that is a different category of activity altogether. I consider work,

---

69. For a good discussion see Witold Rybczynski, *Waiting for the Weekend* (New York: Viking, 1991), 21-26: "'It is commonly believed that happiness depends on leisure' Aristotle wrote in his *Ethics*, 'because we occupy ourselves so that we may have leisure, just as we make war in order that we may have peace.' "Both Russell and Chesterton agreed with Aristotle, who considered leisure the aim of life. 'We work' he wrote, 'in order to have leisure.'" For an even better book on the subject, see Kathryn Grover, ed., *Hard at Play: Leisure in America, 1840-1940* (Amherst, Mass: University of Massachusetts Press, 1992).

or "good work" as Wendell Berry calls it,[70] to be generous service to family and / or community. I don't think the idea of work stands in antagonism to play, nor does it denigrate play's merits. But I do want to reassert the centrality of work in our lives. Let me explain a little.

I consider generosity to be the most important of all virtues, and good work is all about being generous. Playing is doing what you want, in the moment; work is doing what you think you ought to be doing. Which is why I think ideas about child development built on a foundation of play need to be so carefully examined. Some conceptions of freedom are built on individual liberty, but I believe real freedom has to be understood as a social construction. Very often free-schoolers and deschoolers articulate a praxis that involves everyone doing what they want all the time, held in place by only a superstructure of minimal rules for coexistence. This kind of sincere liberalism is appealing in some ways and repugnant in others.

Schools are by their nature isolated (to varying degrees) from larger social contexts, and that is the root of what I am after here. If one were to create a delightful, beautiful institution where children of privilege (those who have access to social resources by way of class, race, education, good parents, charm) were able to find complete liberty to play and develop themselves to their absolute potential, how much freedom would that be? That is to say, freedom cannot be understood as liberty itself, and play is all about liberty, as Jonathan Kozol points out:

> While children starve and others walk the city streets in fear on Monday afternoon, the privileged young people in the Free Schools of Vermont shuttle their handlooms back and forth and speak of love and of "organic processes." They do "their thing." Their thing is sun and good food and fresh

70. Wendell Berry, *Standing By Words: Essays* (San Francisco: North Point, 1983), 73.

water and good doctors and delightful, old, and battered
eighteenth-century houses, and a box of baby turtles; somebody else's thing may be starvation, broken glass, unheated
rooms, and rats inside the bed with newborn children. The
beautiful children do not *wish* cold rooms or broken glass,
starvation, rats, or fear for anybody; nor will they stake their
lives, or put their bodies on the line, or interrupt one hour of
the sunlit morning, or sacrifice one moment of the golden
afternoon, to take a hand in altering the unjust terms of a
society in which these things are possible.[71]

I think a pedagogy that is organized primarily around play, without a careful consideration of what that might mean, can come very
close to the kind of scenario Kozol is pointing to. I realize that I am
interweaving political and pedagogical arguments, but I think with
good reason. The point is that play cannot be so easily disembedded from work, and my experience with children of all ages suggests to me that this is important. It is not about making children
do things "for their own good," nor about canonical formulations.

I am most interested in living in community, and not just in a
school "community," and trying to understand freedom as more
than selfishness. The misuse of the word community is important
to address: an institution like a school is not a community. It can be
a wonderful, caring, supportive, lasting place, but it is an institutional affiliation. A community is a collection of disparate individuals in a place, who are committed to that place. The boundaries
have to be fluid in some senses, but it is about a placed people, to
use a Wendell Berry phrase, and includes the land, water and animals within that place. A school, even the nicest free school, is not
a community — but it may well be part of one.

The danger I see in a praxis built around play is the disembed-

71. Jonathan Kozol, *Free Schools* (New York: Bantam, 1973), 11. Kozol is
certainly sanctimonious, but the power and essential truth of what he says
remain.

ding of *personal* development from any context of *social* development. I appreciate the pedagogical support for playing, for allowing the mind to wander freely, for unfettered exploration. I do believe that people learn best when they are pursuing their own interests and their own passions, and that the social context has to be acknowledged.

I'm interested in perceiving good work as self-driven, generous activity in one's community. It is what a person thinks she *ought* to be doing. Now that opens up another whole can of armchair-psychology worms, because our conceptions, even from our earliest years about what we *should* be doing are obviously socially constructed. Nevertheless, I maintain faith that in an atmosphere of social freedom, where people, whatever their age, are allowed to make real decisions about their time, the distinctions between work and play begin to fade into the same constellation of questions about what constitutes the good life and good living. I have this faith because I see it at work in the non-coercive schools and scenarios I visit and participate in.

I have no interest in the large and growing body of literature that seeks to see more play integrated into the classroom. Reformists have always attempted to cannibalize isolated parts of radical ideals for assimilation into traditional schools.[72] It is important that play's most meaningful qualities be counterposed to manipulative schooling, and that play not be degraded into just another technique at a teacher's disposal:

> I believe that with play, we teachers can have it all . . . Developing curriculum experiences that are rooted in play is not

72. As Selma Wasserman notes in "Serious Play in the Classroom," *Prime Areas* 39, no. 2: 96-97, for example: "The ideas behind serious play have taken root in primary and intermediate classrooms in British Columbia as part of the Ministry of Education's comprehensive education plan. It is gratifying to see just how much curriculum content can be learned through investigative play . . . Serious play is also emerging as a teaching strategy in 'teaching with cases' in B.C. secondary schools as well."

difficult. A successful program, however, requires that certain
conditions be met to ensure that students develop knowledge
and conceptual understanding. 1. The teacher must be able to
design and orchestrate a curriculum rooted in play. [The
author goes on to carefully lay out a curriculum process
model.] . . . The label *Play-Debrief-Replay* describes this curriculum design. It is a way of looking at how curriculum
experiences may be organized.[73]

It doesn't take much insight to see just how much contradiction is
built into this attempt. As teachers and education bureaucrats
reach for the benefits of non-coercive learning, they invariably
pervert it by trying to force it into a compulsory pedagogical environment. You can't allow kids to "follow their interests" *and* force
them to follow an "orchestrated curriculum." It's a mistake I often
find myself making when I ask kids a question I really only want
one answer to. That's not a real question, that's a manipulative
attempt to weasel someone into agreement. Taking something as
noble as "play" and trying to mould it into another technique in
the teacher's tool box is well worth resisting.

◎ ◎ ◎

I believe childhood *should* be about irresponsibility at some level,
that kids *should* be cushioned from some of the real concerns of
the world, such as how the next bill is to be paid. To paraphrase
Gloria Steinem, equality means treating people differently, and the
questions kids ask themselves about work and play should not be
the same ones adults are asking. I have heard it said that "play is
kids' work," and frankly that strikes me as weird. Children's activities should be valued for what they are, not the degree to which
they resemble adults' lives.

   It strikes me that for even for the youngest kids, work and play

73. *Ibid.*, 16, 21.

are hardly distinguishable: they are one and the same thing really. The critical questions about any activity are who is making me do this, and why? There are some obvious distinctions between work and play, but there is a lot more grey area. Is cleaning the house work? How about putting the kids to bed? Is helping a neighbour clean a local park work? How about hanging out with a teenager who is asking for advice? Is work for others and play for ourselves? It is not hard to generate many other examples that demonstrate the degree to which separating work and play is a futile and flawed exercise. Play and work do not exist to augment the other. We do not play so that we can work better (recharging the batteries) or work so that we can play better (working for the weekend), but the two are one and the same, sweeping descriptions of parts of a whole person.

Although I share many of Sadofsky's pedagogical beliefs, I disagree with much of what she writes about play. I do not always "play" when I have the time to (which would suggest work is something I do against my will), and typically I find work at least as satisfactory as play — and often moreso. I simply do not believe that "allowing my mind to roam freely" is how my mind expands best. Often I feel my own learning is maximized in conversation, in confrontations with the Other, a fundamentally very different experience from roaming freely. My most creative moments sometimes come in "playing with new ideas," but they more often come when I am challenged. The equation of work with joylessness is just not my experience, nor that of most of the people around me.

☺ ☺ ☺

I hardly want this chapter to emerge as an assault on the idea of play. There is already far, far too much of that around. I want to celebrate the best parts of play. I do, however, want to caution against some of the ideas being thrown around glibly, especially by deschoolers. I think that discipline, an important and underappreciated ideal, must run through the work / play mix. Discipline, not the willingness to submit to manipulative authority, can only be truly developed through self-direction, an idea that is entwined with the renditions of authority discussed in the previous chapter. John Holt has had much to say about this, and in *Freedom and Beyond* he describes learning how to play the cello later in life:

> So, during those two years, it was my regular custom to get up at about four or four-thirty in the morning, get dressed, pack up my cello, music and music stand, walk to the school, open the building, find an empty room, set up stand and music, and start to practise. When the building began to fill up, around eight o'clock, I would pack up, returning again in the evening, if I was not playing with a group. My friends were baffled by this regime. They didn't know whether to call it work or play. It didn't seem to be work, because no one was making me do it or paying me for it, and there was no other kind of reward or benefit I would get from it. At the same time, they couldn't think of it as play — how can anyone call "play" getting up at four and walking through dark winter streets just to practise for three hours.[74]

In the end, there is much to be said for play. I am very interested in children being unburdened by worry and tension. I love the idea of kids being able to play all day every day, especially when the rendition of play is one that is inseparable from work. If work and play are understood as inadequate descriptions of activity, and if people of all ages are constantly asking themselves not only what they want to do but what they think they ought to do, then I am all for "play."

74. John Caldwell Holt, *Freedom and Beyond* (New York: Dutton, 1972), 108.

Helen Hughes

Helen Hughes was born and raised in British Columbia. She married at nineteen and taught elementary school for five years. She then trained as a preschool teacher when her children were young and had her eyes opened by the curiosity and integrity of four- and five-year-olds, compared with the jaded and resistant twelve-year-olds she taught in schools. In 1971, when her daughter, then in Grade 2, began to lose her spirit, Hughes gathered a group of parents and started a fifteen-student school in their house on Windsor Road in North Vancouver. The school grew and changed, Hughes had another baby, and they ran out of funds. The school appealed to the North Vancouver School Board, which took the school over and hired Hughes to teach.

Windsor House slowly grew to about sixty-five students and was moved to a new location every five years. When the school was twenty years old, Hughes became ill for two years and the school dwindled to seventeen students. When she returned to work, Hughes began rebuilding the school as openly non-coercive. The school moved to its present location in North Vancouver and began to grow in size. For the past ten years, Windsor House has taken in older students (up to eighteen years old) and has grown to 200 students. Helen retired

at the end of the 2002–2003 school year and will continue
learning at Windsor House. She has big plans to build a fort
in the upper forest.

In your experience, how long has it been that people have
been talking about "play" as an educational tool, as useful
to a child's upbringing?

At least forty years. I taught public school for five years
and then I went and taught preschool and kindergarten, and
took some training, and was stunned by what they were
teaching to these young children because it was totally different from what my teacher training had been six years earlier. This was in the early sixties, and that's when I first got
the idea that play could be so valuable. They were talking
about it for very young kids, using all the academic jargon,
correlating every play activity to some academic skill, while
none of that was being discussed for school-age children, it
was just "pour it in."

What role do you see play having in your larger educational
praxis?

I think, and most people will surely not agree with me,
that children should pretty well play most of the time until
about the age of twelve. I think that the value of play is far
different than the kinds of academic correlations some people might want to make, using measuring spoons to learn
fractions and all that kind of stuff. That's not what I see as
the value of play. I think play is laying down the actual experiences that your body and mind can take in and not forget.
The things you do in play you don't forget because they are
not necessarily even conscious. You just have these experiences, so you notice what happens when liquid comes up a
straw, when you shake off a blanket, when you pick up
something that you thought was heavy but was light . . . a
zillion different experiences.

When astronauts need to learn how to manage without
gravity, they play with moving their bodies, lifting things,

pouring liquids and much more. As they play, their bodies learn how to cope.

And after twelve . . . they should work?

That's a good distinction, because when I use the word "play" there I am actually thinking of playing with *real things*, instead of abstract ideas. Twelve is a very general number. Quite often girls are ready to move into abstract thinking at a younger age than that, while for many boys it's a lot older, but it is somewhere in there. It becomes clear, or at least it does at Windsor House, when a child is ready for abstract thinking because they start going to events and classes where they are just sitting and talking. Everything they talk about they have to have had some kind of experience because talking about something abstract that you have no experience with, it doesn't actually mean anything to you. Once there is a base of experience, then it is possible to make abstract intellectual jumps.

Why do so many parents want to see their kids work so much? I talked to a parent yesterday who said he just wanted to see his daughter "put her nose to the grindstone." Why does the idea of kids playing a lot piss people off so much?

I think it pisses them off because a lot of people hate their jobs. It's hard to see other people not hating what they are doing.

I see a few levels of development. At first, children play with real things. Then, given the opportunity, they start to play with abstract things whenever they are ready. Ideally, they can earn their living doing things that mostly seem like play to them. I like to see people working hard at things they like to do and things that are meaningful to them.

So how would you begin to define play? Or work?

Just interacting with whatever you have in your environment and using your imagination and your own ideas with or without others is my idea of play. It also has to be a chosen activity. I don't see a big difference between work and play, because in my life what I'm paid for as work feels like play to me. I've never had a horrendous job. Everything I have ever done for employment I've enjoyed doing. Even the difficult times, the long, tedious meetings, have always fascinated me. It wasn't that they were wonderful, it's that I wanted to be there.

My life has been mostly play, but I work hard at it.

I'm not clear on this, but how about this for a distinction. Play is what you want to do in the moment, acting imaginatively, creatively, spontaneously. Work is what you think you ought to do, what you want to do looking at the larger picture. Play is a certain kind of self-centredness, while work is for a greater good.

I wonder if you could say that work is what you have to do (or choose to say you have to do), while play is what you choose to do.

I think that work and play are mixed in together all the time. One morphs into the other, and I don't think there are hard lines between the two. I have never read a definition that satisfies me.

I think that's right. Maybe they are like Platonic ideals, and all activity has elements of both . . . although now that I say that, it doesn't sound true . . .

What I am in favour of is people being actively engaged in activities of their own choice.

Do you think it possible that a pedagogy that supports kids playing all day might run the danger of inculcating selfish personalities?

I just don't see that in the people around me. That's not what I observe. I observe kids who are left to choose what it is that they are doing maturing into fine, responsible people, over and over again.

Do you think that allowing kids to do what they want to do, to play all day long, creates a kind of social vacuum where dominant culture can rush in?

I am more inclined to tell kids what they can't do than what they can. I'd like it if families said "no" to television, and "no, you can't go to the mall all day. Think of something else to do." I don't want play to mean free rein.

To me, play means becoming engaged, usually with other people, but not always, and with your surroundings. As kids get older that can evolve into playing with ideas and abstractions. I think there are various kinds of play and I don't think that everything people are doing on their own is play. My definition of play includes creativity. Kids sitting around insulting each other isn't play, that's just being at loose ends. It's where boredom defaults to.

You've heard the line "play is child's work." A.S. Neill said that "every moment of a healthy child's life is a working moment." What do you make of that?

I think it means that you are doing important, real stuff when you are playing. That play matters the same way people think work matters. That's all.

Free schools are trying to describe a way to live in the world, trying to describe a "good life." State schools describe a way to live in the world that they expect children to mimic once they leave: accepting authority, rewards and punishments, taking orders, central guidance and all the rest.

Do you expect kids to move in the world the way they move at Windsor House?

Yes, I do. In fact, I have been moving Windsor House towards a model of being a resource rather like a library, only with activities and classes being offered, and with places for groups to gather. This resource would be for people of all ages.

I think it would be very preferable if people could find a way to earn their living doing things that give them satisfaction, and that their energy comes up for. Your life can become a blend of work and play of your own choosing, understanding that you are choosing to be in a particular milieu, not choosing every little activity.

I expect kids who come through a school like this to go on in their lives and do things that I would never dream of. I think that while they are here they experience the kinds of behaviours and actions that they will continue to use in the world at large, but they will exceed what they do here. Play and work are the raw materials they can use.

For example, there is a group of kids here who get huge satisfaction from building forts, which has elements of both work and play. They work at their play. They are clearly playing at fort building, and they are working hard.

This is another good example. When you are little and you are going to build a fort in the living room, and you run around the house and gather blankets and pillows and every-thing, and the whole time you are doing it, it doesn't take you any effort. You don't have to push yourself, it flows like magic and your energy is right up. Then it is time to put it all away and your energy drops like a stone, and it is a hard, onerous task to put it away. It is the exact reverse of what you just did so easily. It is just the way it is viewed. It becomes a completely different thing.

The more of your life you can lead that has that fort-building energy, the better.

Pedagogy and Freedom

Up to this point I've tossed around a fair number of assumptions about how kids thrive in places where their freedom is considered seriously. I think it's worth looking a little more closely at this here, specifically at how the everyday experience of freedom makes sense both to and with children.

A good place to start is with George Dennison, who in one short book, *The Lives of Children*, said more good things about kids than whole university education departments do in decades. Talking about freedom, Dennison writes:

> The question is not really one of authority, though it is usually argued in that form. When adults give up authority, the freedom of children is not necessarily increased. Freedom is not motion in a vacuum, but motion in a continuum. If we want to know what freedom is, we must discover what the continuum is . . . it is another name for the fullness and final shape of activities. We experience the activities, not the freedom. The mother of a child in public school told me that he kept complaining that "they never let me *finish* anything!" We might say of the child that he lacked important freedoms, but his own expression is closer to the experience: activities important to him remained unfulfilled. Our concern for freedom is our concern for fulfillment — of activities we deem important and of persons we know are unique.[75]

I think this begins to bring things into a little more focus. The practice of freedom cannot be disembedded from lived life, nor reduced to the two-dimensionality of "choice." Freedom is much fuller and has to mean *experience*. It has to be understood as social context, and kids practising freedom is about them learning how to move in shifting and complex circumstances:

75. George Dennison, *The Lives of Children: The Story of the First Street School* (New York: Vintage, 1969), 4.

The proper concern of a primary school is not education in a narrow sense, and still less preparation for later life, but the present lives of children . . .

Let me replace the word "freedom" with more specific terms: 1) we trusted that some true organic bond existed between the wishes of children and their actual needs, and 2) we acceded to their wishes (though certainly not to all of them), and thus encouraged their childish desiring to take on the qualities of decision-making . . .

The huge school does not create diversity of experience; it creates anonymity and anxiety . . . among twenty-three children, under conditions of freedom and respect, there is a true abundance of experience. It is experience in depth, and it leads to decisive change.[76]

It's that "abundance of experience" that is so critical to freedom. A healthy life, especially for kids, is all about doing stuff; actively engaging the world instead of being acted upon. I'm not talking about activities with larger educational intents that are designed and planned for the participants' own good, but working with materials, meeting people, building, writing, painting, hiking, playing or anything for experience itself. It is unmediated experience, people directly engaging the world around them, that is raw material people build their lives out of. Deprived of direct experience in schools, kids have far too little to actually fashion themselves with.

The pedagogies that drive what is now called "experiential education" are frequently emblematic of the manipulative intent of educators: taking something so simple as a hike or a camping trip and insisting on trying to fashion the experience, determine the value and direct the learning for participants "for their own good." Why can't lived experience be the material that people work with? Why do professionals feel compelled to mediate everything?

76. *Ibid.*, 21-22.

This is hardly to denigrate abstract thinking because I think kids of all ages want to engage in intellectual discourse and thought — including abstract thought — but we all need an abundance of unmediated experience to make sense of the world and to contextualize abstract ideas. Our culture has restricted kids' ability to directly engage with the world at large to an alarming degree. Many children are in daycare from very early in their lives until they reach kindergarten, and then they spend the bulk of their next thirteen years isolated in classrooms. Without that deep reservoir of direct experience, ideas have trouble adhering to anything in particular and float free. The result is a fractured understanding of the world that so many teachers speak of their students possessing, an inability to grasp even the rudiments of geography or history, or to place themselves in a larger world.

Speaking of freedom and children has to be talking about how kids can engage with the world around them, to build that reservoir of experience. The impetus has to be the inherent curiosity all kids have for the world, the desire to be part of it and do things. I don't want to hear that this is flaky hyperbole. I think it can definitely be asserted that all kids have this innate curiosity. It can be dulled through abuse, neglect, endless exposure to TV or a grim upbringing, but a desire to learn and investigate the world is something everyone is born with. The insistence by educators and parents on finding pedagogies, learning tools, teachable moments, educationally appropriate toys, useful videos and curriculum-supporting books invariably does little but get in the way of children's capacity to understand their world. Adults would do well just to *be* with the kids around them, to do exciting and interesting things with them, to follow their interests, and simply to live well.

The drive to educate is an "original sin" kind of impulse, a belief that without trained, professional assistance, children will forever remain ignorant. It's something that Ivan Illich has pointed out often:

By the early seventeenth century a new consensus began to arise: the idea that man was born incompetent for society and remained so unless he was provided with "education." Education came to mean the inverse of vital competence. It came to mean a process rather than the plain knowledge of the facts and the ability to use tools which shape a man's concrete life. Education came to mean an intangible commodity that had to be produced for the benefit of all, and imparted to them in the manner in which the visible Church formerly imparted invisible grace. Justification in the sight of society became the first necessity for a man born in original stupidity, analogous to original sin.[77]

Absolutely *every* child wants to grow up well: no one hopes or dreams of being stupid or ignorant or lazy or incompetent. The practice of freedom is living with kids every day, not moulding them or guiding them, but being with them and supporting them in meaningful activities, taking them seriously, letting them blur play and work, and more than anything, letting them act in the world.

Children learn from anything and everything they see. They learn wherever they are, not just in special learning places. They learn much more from things, natural or made, that are real and significant in the world in their own right and not just made in order to help children learn . . .

We can best help children learn, not by deciding what we think they should learn and thinking of ingenious ways to teach it to them, but by making the world, as far as we can, accessible to them, paying serious attention to what they do, answering their questions — if they have any — and helping them explore the things they are most interested in.[78]

77. Ivan Illich, *Toward a History of Needs* (Berkeley: Heyday, 1977), 75-76.
78. Holt, *Learning All the Time*, 162.

I don't mean here that I expect adults who are around children to "get out of the way," which is a phrase I hear deschoolers use sometimes. I don't think adults should be afraid to speak their minds around kids, or tone down their natural authority, or mute their personalities. I think adults should be who they are, should articulate their values and joys, should be in a real relationship with kids. Authority and freedom are not scarce resources and adults do not have to lose theirs for kids to gain them. Children do not need weak, suppressed or obsequious people around. They need caring adults who don't pawn them off on professionals at the first opportunity. They need adults who will listen to them, treat them and their interests seriously and will not underestimate what kids are capable of.

> I have been urging one simple truth through all these pages: the educational function does not rest upon our ability to control or our will to instruct, but upon our human nature and the nature of experience.[79]

Developing an atmosphere free of coercion won't necessarily help kids thrive, but a commitment to freedom makes it possible. Some people flourish in constrained and constricted scenarios, but only if they are there of their own accord. My own classes, for example, whether with small children or in a university scenario, are often very structured. I do not teach, I lecture, and I usually want to get down to it. I am sincere about what I want to say, and I want people there to be sincere as well. Demanding a focused and sustained atmosphere is completely consistent with a non-coercive institution. It is only agreement, not compulsion, that can legitimately bind people.

No one has ever described how it is that children learn best, though so many have tried and continue to try as if it were a tech-

79. Dennison, *Lives of Children*, 246.

nical quandary to be cracked. It is literally impossible to describe how another person learns best, and it's absurd arrogance to believe that it can be described en masse.

As Illich puts it, it is a "'pedagogical hubris' which seeks to replace the perpetual but unpredictable possibility of learning with a certified process based on the pretension that 'Man can do what God cannot, namely manipulate others for their own salvation'."[80]

The question of learning and freedom cannot be a consideration of whether or not free circumstances "work," but how it is that people came to believe they could be disconnected.

80. Cayley, *Ivan Illich in Conversation*, 10.

Photo Essay

by Richard Lawley

3 A Schooled Culture

Out of her pocket Pippi took a lovely little gold watch and laid it on the desk. The teacher said she couldn't possibly accept such a valuable gift from Pippi, but Pippi replied, "You've got to take it; otherwise I'll come back again tomorrow, and that would be a pretty how-do-you-do."

Then Pippi rushed out to the schoolyard and jumped on her horse. All the children gathered around to pat the horse and see her off.[81]

What Is an Educated Person?

The question of what makes an educated person has become a major battleground over the past forty years and is worth addressing clearly here. At some point before that it may have been much clearer what constituted "educated," but that is most certainly not the case now.

For the past four decades, and largely driven by emerging identity movements (feminists, Latin Americans, African and Native Americans, gay and lesbian rights activists, ecologists and many, many more), traditional interpretations of what someone needs to

81. Lindgren, *Pippi Longstocking*, 59.

know have come under heavy challenge. Universities and grade schools alike have been challenged to include marginalized perspectives and alternative viewpoints and to embrace a certain degree of relativism. Now post-secondary institutions commonly offer degrees in Women's Studies, Afro-American Studies and Environmental Science. High schools rarely leave Columbus as the discoverer of America any longer. Not only has the form of education come under attack, but the everyday content as well.

Thus, in the opening years of the twenty-first century, education itself — not just its delivery — remains a major battleground between liberals and conservatives of all predilections. Liberals tend to argue for the widening of curricula and the inclusion of varying viewpoints. Conservatives tend to rail against the "watering down" of education, the denigration of basic skills and knowledges. The question that I want to ask, though, is whether education is even a goal worth considering, or a delusion worth abandoning.

In the late 1800s, as universal education programs had been widely adopted in both Europe and the U.S., Russian anarchist Leo Tolstoy made distinctions between teaching and learning, education and culture. "Education is the tendency of one man to make another just like himself. Education is culture under restraint. Culture is free."[82]

A century later, Tolstoy's words are echoed often. In *Instead of Education* John Holt writes that he is:

> In favour of *doing* — self-directed, purposeful, meaningful life and work — and *against* "education" — learning cut off from active life and done under pressure of bribe or threat, greed and fear . . .
>
> I choose to define [education] here as most people do, something that people do to others for their own good, moulding and shaping them, and trying to make them learn what they

82. Leo Tolstoy, quoted in Peter Marshall, *A History of Anarchism* (London: Fontana, 1993), 365.

think they ought to know. Today, everywhere in the world, that is what "education" has become, and I am wholly against it.[83]

Aaron Falbel echoes and builds on both Tolstoy and Holt:

> Today our social environment is thoroughly polluted by *education* — a designed process in which one group of people (educators, social engineers, people shapers) tries to make another group (those who are to be "educated") learn something, usually without their consent, because they (the "educators") think it will be good for them. In other words, education is forced, seduced or coerced learning — except that you can't really make a person learn something he or she doesn't want to learn, which is why education doesn't work *and has never worked*. People have always learned things, but *education* is a relatively recent invention, and a deeply destructive one at that.[84]

I really do believe that there is a broad understanding that education is a process that is necessarily other-designed and -directed. In *Keywords*, Raymond Williams outlined the historical progression of the word "educated", moving from its etymological roots, *educare* (to rear or to foster), to a wider sense of organized teaching and instruction:

> When a majority of children had such organized instruction the distinction between *educated* and *uneducated* was reasonably clear, but, curiously, this distinction has been more common since the development of generally organized education and even of universal education. There is a strong class sense in this use, and the level indicated by *educated* has been continuously adjusted to leave the majority of people who have received an education below it . . .

83. Holt, *Instead of Education*, 3.
84. Aaron Falbel, "Learning? Yes, of Course. Education? No, Thanks," in *Deschooling Our Lives*, ed. Matt Hern, 66.

> It remains remarkable that after nearly a century of universal education in Britain the majority of the population should in this use be seen as *uneducated* or *half-educated*, but whether *educated people* think of this with self-congratulation or self-reproach, or with impatience at the silliness of the usage, is for them to say.[85]

I think "educated" might mean knowing what one needs to know to grow up right — an ideal that is hegemonically driven in schools. It invokes a measure of participatory membership, that if you are willing to become educated then you have completed the prerequisites for entering into the larger cultural discourse, except that a majority of people are always excluded. Which is part of why education is such a battleground.

The liberal-conservative debate as to what people need to know centres on the *canon*. The canon is that body of knowledge that is required in order to be educated. The amount of knowledge that can be contained within the canon obviously cannot expand endlessly, so anything added necessarily displaces something else. For example, when activists insist that First Nations viewpoints be included in legitimate historical renditions of the resettlement of North America, those viewpoints must displace former interpretations.

Clifford Geertz has famously described culture as "the ensemble of stories we tell ourselves about ourselves,"[86] and education is all about which stories get told. Do your kids, for example, need to know that Columbus discovered America, or should they know what the experience was for the people who had been living in North America for millennia? What rendition of the European / First Nations intersection do they need to hear? When liberals and conservatives address this question, it is in the context of public,

85. Raymond Williams, *Keywords: A Vocabulary of Culture and Society* (London: Fontana, 1976), 112.
86. Clifford Geertz, quoted in Ziauddin Sardar and Borin Van Loon, *Introducing Cultural Studies* (Cambridge: Icon, 1999), 5.

compulsory education and the instruction of millions and millions of children, which makes for rather high stakes. These questions also have very intense financial implications for the hordes who make their money from textbooks, school workshops and curriculum development.

The real purpose of educative distinctions may well be the maintenance of class and social divisions, because if it is clear what "educated" is, it must also be clear what "uneducated" is.

> Our first task is to realize that an "uneducated" human being is nowhere to be found. But today, all too often, an ordinary schoolboy treats a first-class carpenter as if he were an ignorant boor. The carpenter may be a man of maturity and experience, a wise and skilled workman, who is of real service to his community. But simply because he cannot read or write, the "educated" boy treats him as an inferior.[87]

Once larger standards are established as to what constitutes an educated person, it necessarily derides the experience and abilities of those who fall outside them. Mass compulsory schooling is always to the detriment of local knowledge, because it relies on a universalizing logic, and the ideal of "educated" cannot be left to the enigmatic, fluid and variegated interpretations the term *educare* implies. When state schooling is universalized, the idea of education is solidified and becomes bureaucratized, and coercive education overrides local distinctions: this is globalization at work.

◎ ◎ ◎

In response to contemporary liberal educational reforms attacking both the content and delivery of education, many layers of conservative response have developed. Perhaps the most important and influential incarnation of this tendency is what is called the core

---

87. Bhave, *The Intimate and the Ultimate*, 18-19.

knowledge movement. Spurred by the writings of people like Harold Bloom, Allan Bloom and Dinesh D'Souza,[88] and centred on the work of E.D. Hirsch,[89] core knowledge proposals claim that American schools are failing to deliver a content-based curriculum, delivering instead a miseducation that is shutting public school students out from larger cultural conversations.

Hirsch's central argument in *Cultural Literacy: What Every American Needs to Know* is built around his conception of a national culture.[90] Hirsch, a University of Virginia English professor, believes that the U.S. is held together by a common cultural heritage, a shared body of knowledge that defines and creates America. He argues that if schools are not instructing their students in the fundamental aspects of this heritage children will be denied the possibility of engaging in the critical conversations that by definition draw on this heritage. Hirsch argues against "content-neutral" curricula that focus on learning processes, critical-thinking skills, problem-solving and self-esteem building. He believes that children have a hugely underestimated ability to absorb information and factual data, and that American education should be primarily about passing on as much of the national heritage as possible. Beyond that, *Cultural Literacy* claims that not only are educators failing children in general, they are failing poor children especially, ensuring they remain marginalized because without an essential knowledge base to work from and with, students are denied the chance to engage the larger culture.

88. See for examples, Allan Bloom, *The Closing of the American Mind* (New York: Simon and Schuster, 1987); Harold Bloom, *The Western Canon: The Books and School of the Ages* (New York: Harcourt Brace, 1994) and *How to Read and Why* (New York: Scribner, 2000); and Dinesh D'Souza, *Illiberal Education: The Politics of Race and Sex on Campus* (New York: Free Press, 1991).
89. E.D. Hirsch is himself extending a well-trod argument, see for example Terry Eagleton, *Literary Theory: An Introduction* (Minneapolis: University of Minnesota Press, 1996).
90. E.D. Hirsch, *Cultural Literacy: What Every American Needs to Know* (Boston: Houghton Mifflin, 1987).

Hirsch is unambiguous about what should and should not be included in this basic knowledge base and proceeds to list its contents. The book's subtitle *What Every American Needs to Know*, offers a clue that this is not an exclusively theoretical piece. Hirsch concludes with a master list: he starts with numbers; 1066, 1492, 1776, etcetera, and swiftly moves to the A's, working his way alphabetically and comprehensively: abbreviation, abolitionism, abominable snowman, abortion, Abraham and Isaac and so on.

Since then, running uphill against a hailstorm of furious attacks by those who view his core knowledge lists as absurdly Westernized, white and male, Hirsch and his Core Knowledge Foundation have proceeded to put out a series of comprehensive curricula for children, beginning with *What Your First Grader Needs to Know*[91] and moving up through the grades.

The Core Knowledge Foundation not only produces texts, but also supports more than a hundred member schools across America with books, teaching materials, consulting services and curricular development. It attempts to give member schools the raw material necessary to transcend any confusion about what is important:

> Objectors have said that traditional materials are class-bound, white, Anglo-Saxon, and Protestant, not to mention racist, sexist, and excessively Western. Our schools have tried to offer enough diversity to meet these objections from liberals and enough Shakespeare to satisfy conservatives. Caught between ideological parties, the schools have acted irresistibly to a quantitative and formal approach to curriculum making rather than one based on sound judgment about what should be taught.[92]

91. E.D. Hirsch, *What Your First Grader Needs to Know* (New York: Doubleday, 1991).
92. Hirsch, *Cultural Literacy*, 21.

Hirsch is attempting to clarify what should be taught and in what sequence, and he makes no apologies for what he considers "national literate culture." Hirsch's ideas are precisely what Plato intended and form the chief inspiration of the core knowledge movement.

I detail core knowledge proposals so carefully here because they represent the most compelling and considered defence of traditional compulsory schooling I know of. Hirsch's arguments are critical to engage because they speak far more truthfully and directly than those of most "for your own good" liberal educators. Core knowledge proposals are merely crystalizing and illuminating the ideas that compulsory schooling has always been based on. At heart, monopoly schooling is all about citizen production and national maintenance, just as Plato ("education for Plato was the means by which the philosopher-king could shape human nature in order to produce a harmonious state . . ."[93]) first described two and a half millennia ago. Hirsch echoes the Platonic imperatives not to allow education and the care of children to become too fractured or diversified in the hands of private interests, lest central social control be lost irrevocably.

Hirsch and core knowledge proponents are making a pedagogical argument about schools, schooling and education, but the *political* implications and basis for his work are plainly obvious. In many ways Hirsch is best at laying out just what is at stake here, and there is a lot. By reasserting the need for a national curriculum and culture, and the primacy of national heritage that is commonly and constantly referenced, Hirsch is attempting to solidify where cultural and social power rests.

The fundamental point here is *not* what is in the canon. It strikes me as specifically obscurantist to debate what people should or should not know. The real question is whether or not there is a

93. Fisher, *Classical Utopian Theories of Education*, 28.

canon at all: whether or not a canon, however defined, can or should exist.

If one believes that the state should be critically involved in child-rearing, that the state should define what *educated* is and that schools are acknowledged as citizen / worker production centres, then describing a canon starts to makes sense. Given that stance, *education* is necessarily about moulding a coherent population that will share common ideals, presumptions and heritage. On the other hand, if we understand education to mean something other than people-shaping, or we reject the ideological constraints of coherent national standards, or we believe people develop and learn best in enigmatic and non-systematic ways, then the idea of a canon is deeply problematic — not in its content but in its very formulation.

◎ ◎ ◎

I have no interest in advocating for a content-weak philosophy of child-rearing — the reverse, actually, and I agree that children have a hugely underestimated ability to absorb data and information and are capable of far more than schools understand. Core knowledge, though, is heading in exactly the wrong direction. I look at Hirsch's lists or typical school curricula, and all the information on it seems useful stuff for people to know. I would like it if my own kids and all the kids I work with could completely grasp every item on those lists. Hell, I would like it if I knew all that was on those lists, even the third-grader ones.

I am not willing, though, to concede that those lists should be central to *anyone* but E.D. Hirsch's understanding of what one needs to know. There are innumerable other lists that could and should be generated describing useful skills and knowledges, if that could possibly be a useful exercise. The attempt to standardize, centralize and prescribe for millions is simultaneously reductive and deeply arrogant.

The project of bringing children up into the public sphere and transmitting culture is an immensely complex and variegated process that lies right at the heart of conceptions about the good life. It is only individuals and those close to them who have legitimate authority to speak on what they need to know to grow up right. I can imagine concentric circles of authority, with the individual in the centre, family and close friends next and friends and associates next, with power decreasing the farther one gets from the centre. An aging, conservative professor of English at the University of Virginia is in a distant circle for the vast majority of the population.

The closer one looks at the concept of an *educated* person, the more it becomes evident that its most salient and lasting purpose is in defining its opposite. That is, those who want to define an educated person are really attempting to identify those who are *uneducated*, with all its implications of social hierarchy and control.

> I began to speak about education as learning under the assumption that the means for this purpose are scarce. If I had only one desire, it would be to get across to the people who study education, researchers *on* education, that they should study not what happens *in* education, but how the *very idea* of this nonsense could have come into existence.[94]

The more we allow compulsory education to dominate key aspects of everyday lives, especially in the guise of schooling, the more we accept the social stratification that it embeds.

The Control of Children

It wouldn't be too much of a stretch to argue that the history of schooling is one long examination into the ways children can be

94. Cayley, *Ivan Illich in Conversation*, 209.

best controlled. At a root level, schools have to be about ware-housing kids, just keeping them off the streets and out of the way while adult life goes on. "Stay in School" mantras are obviously not just about what is best for kids, but also about what adults want and *don't* want themselves.

I have spoken at length already of how school pedagogies have always been institutionally driven; that is, kids are expected to adapt (sometimes radically) to fit institutions, not the other way round. Within that construct there is a wide debate around spe-cific control approaches: how best to make students learn faster, sit down, keep quiet, stop fiddling and quit skipping, and how to make them less obnoxious, abusive, resistant and / or willful.

For the most part, those discourses have been essentially tech-nology- and / or technique-driven, which may or may not amount to the same thing.[95] Emerging alongside the rise of compulsory schooling has been a constellation of industries that are devoted to the control of children: drugs, learning diseases, teaching tech-niques, crowd-control theories, behaviouralism, punishments and rewards, organizational theory and, more recently, various digital or "virtual" proposals for the enhancement / extension of school-ing. Dennison says, "We speak increasingly of control, as if we feared that everything would collapse into nothing if we let loose our (illusory) hold on things."[96]

Conceptions of control are mostly rooted in competing rendi-tions of authority and, now more than ever, marked by an

95. One of my favourite definitions of technology comes from Ursula Franklin, *The Real World of Technology* (Toronto: CBC Enterprises, 1990), 15-16: Franklin, echoing Jacques Ellul among others, describes technology as a system, or following the suggestion of Kenneth Boulding, technology as practice: "as ways of doing something . . . there is a technology of prayer as well as of ploughing . . . The historical process of defining a group by their agreed practice and by their tools is a powerful one." It is certainly a way of considering technology, technique and tools that makes some sense here and rightly blurs some of the distinctions.
96. Dennison, *The Lives of Children*, 246.

increased reliance on technology. Maybe the clearest example of this is the use of psychoactive drugs (primarily, but hardly exclusively, Ritalin) to solve the quandary of overactive / inattentive students, a technological attempt to answer social questions. The number of children being treated pharmaceutically is difficult to pin down and constantly growing:

> Estimates vary anywhere from six to over eight million American children and the figure continues to skyrocket, increasing 23 percent between 1995 and 1999, according to IMS Health. During this brief period the number of kids under the age of eighteen taking the antidepressant Prozac rose 74 percent; between the ages of seven and twelve, 151 percent; and under age six, 580 percent.[97]

It some ways it is useful to think of schools as a technology in themselves: a system of techniques for interceding between kids and the adults or community around them. State schools are explicitly designed to save people from the trouble of having to comprehend (as complicated and difficult a process as that is) what their kids need to thrive. It solves the whole issue about how kids might grow up right by providing one mass answer: they go to school for their entire youth. That's all there is to it. Let the government cover that off.

Schools pose themselves as a technological answer to a project that lies right at the heart of human life: child-rearing. I want to look specifically at the rise of learning diseases and behavioural drugs as an everyday example of the logic of control. The explosive growth of prescribed drug use in schools is an explicit acknowledgment that schools cannot pull off the comprehensive control of children they have claimed is possible.

The heavy use of psychoactive drugs relies on the broad diagnoses of learning disabilities. Straight up, I do not believe that

97. Chris Mercogliano, interview with the author.

learning diseases like attention deficit disorder exist, in the same way that I do not believe there is such a thing as a "gifted" child. I have worked with literally thousands of children in all kinds of scenarios and I have yet to see either of these. I do not dispute in any way that there is a vast range of human learning experience, style, predilection and performance. That is unquestionable, but I fully dispute that anyone can take the whole scope of human variation, learning or otherwise, and partition off learning disabilities. I also do not dispute that certain individuals may exhibit tendencies or behaviours that resemble one another and may be coped with and approached in similar ways. Still, that doesn't reduce similar behaviour, no matter how puzzling, to a learning disease.

This argument is analogous in many ways to the growing body of literature refuting the biological existence of "race."[98] It is an everyday, constant reality that people are racialized with devastating consequences, but the attempt to categorize the entire continuous range of human biological variation into races is a capricious project that has only been attempted in the last four hundred years. The implications of racializing are staggering, and the attempt to reduce individual quirk, differentiation and tendency to disability shares a similar logic.

While attention deficit disorder (ADD) and attention deficit hyperactivity disorder (ADHD) are relatively recent inventions, they are only current manifestations of the long-running attempt to medicalize inattention, restlessness and impulsiveness. Throughout the twentieth century various names have been given to these behaviours, including "organic drivenness," "restlessness syndrome,"

---

98. See for example Richard Lewontin, *The Triple Helix: Gene, Organism and Environment* (Cambridge: Harvard University Press, 2000); Lewontin *et al.*, *Not in Our Genes: Biology, Ideology and Human Nature* (New York: Pantheon, 1984); and Joseph Graves, *The Emperor's New Clothes: Biological Theories of Race at the Millennium* (New Brunswick, N.J.: Rutgers University Press, 2001).

"postencephalitic disorder," "Strauss syndrome," "minimal brain dysfunction," "hyperactive child syndrome" and "hyperkinesis." ADD was given the official seal of approval in 1980 by the American Psychiatric Association, which agreed to classify it as a disorder just as it had regarded homosexuality as a disease until 1974.[99]

Throughout the ensuing years, the American Medical Association's *Diagnostic and Statistical Manual of Mental Disorders* has continuously expanded those characteristics that may be seen as "symptoms" of attention deficit disorder so that more and more children fall under the guidelines. Currently upwards of 8 percent of American and Canadian children have been diagnosed (that's a very low-end estimate; many professionals place the percentages in double digits, especially for boys), while many more fall under the various other definitional boundaries. The symptoms can include fidgeting, inappropriate running, leaving one's seat repeatedly, blurting out answers, impatience, interrupting, forgetfulness and frequently misplacing things. There is no lab test available for diagnoses and it remains a subjective distinction, most often relying heavily on teacher assessments.

More dubious than its diagnostic pattern is the scattershot and arbitrary application of the ADD label. It has now been ascertained that the disorder can manifest itself in certain circumstances, but not in others, which is a facile and transparent way to avoid institutional analysis.

> A physician mother of a child labelled ADD wrote to me not long ago about her frustration with this protean diagnosis: "When I . . . began pointing out to people that my child is capable of long periods of concentration when he is watching his favourite sci-fi video or examining the inner workings of a pin-tumble lock, I notice that next year's definition states that

99. See Thomas Armstrong, *The Myth of the ADD Child* (New York: Dutton, 1995), 8-9.

some kids with ADD are capable of normal attention in certain specific circumstances. Poof! A few thousand more kids
instantly fall into the definition."[100]

More than that, ADD children often do not exhibit *any* of the
symptoms in certain environments, are frequently indistinguish-
able from non-diagnosed children when pursuing activities of their
own choosing and at least half of them have the disorder simply
fall away. This drive to identify inappropriate behaviour specifically excludes the school or classroom from any critical analyses.

It is in keeping with tradition that schools deem children unac-
ceptable if they do not fit in, conform to authority or exhibit standardized behaviour. The attempt to drug a huge swath of children
simply because they won't listen to the teacher, sit down and / or
shut up when told, or display the expected level of docility is out-
rageous — and it continues unabated. Listen to these lines written
almost thirty years ago, in a book called the *Myth of the Hyperactive Child*:

> In the past five years there has been a profound shift in the way
> Americans and American institutions treat children. The shift
> is pervasive, yet so subtle and complex that no simple label is
> adequate. Drawing on hard medical evidence that a small per-
> centage of the population suffers from brain damage or other
> neurological or emotional problems, schools, doctors and ju-
> venile authorities have begun to attribute similar or related
> "ailments" to millions of children who suffer from no scientif-
> ically demonstrable ailments but whose behaviour is regarded
> as troublesome to adults. At the same time — and partly as a
> result — traditional methods of management and control
> (threats, punishment, school suspensions) have been replaced
> by an accumulation of psychosocial and psychochemical tech-

100. *Ibid.*, 13.

niques and by an ideology of "early intervention" which re-
gards almost every form of undesirable behaviour, however benign, as a medical ailment requiring treatment.[101]

These same lines might be replicated almost exactly in contemporary analyses of ADD, and while much remains the same, some
things have certainly changed. Now professionals speak of diseases and disorders, not ailments, but the diagnoses remain firmly
rooted in biological / psychological deficiencies. The scope is
wider and the treatments more intrusive, but the same patterns
and tendencies that were noted in 1975 thrive.

◎ ◎ ◎

When looking at the rate of Ritalin prescription and learning disorder diagnoses, much of the responsibility is directed at teachers.
In some respects this is warranted. Children today (overwhelmingly boys) are being fed Ritalin, along with a whole host of
amphetamines and other drugs, for the simple reason that they
won't consistently fit in with classroom expectations. A typical
pattern is this: a kid enrolls in school, won't sit down, won't stop
moving, won't stop talking and the teacher, understandably, gets
frustrated, calls the parents and they make a preliminary assessment of some kind of disorder. The kid is then seen by a psycholo-
gist who, often on the basis of reports from the teacher, agrees that
it is ADD or ADHD and prescribes a drug treatment plan.

Given this pattern, many see teachers as the root problem. The
argument is that if teachers would be more patient, understanding,
flexible and innovative in their classroom management, then
vastly fewer children would end up dosed. There is some truth to

101. Peter Schrag and Diane Divoky, *The Myth of the Hyperactive Child:
And Other Means of Child Control* (New York: Pantheon, 1975), 1.

this. That many teachers would rather go to the drug cabinet than tackle difficult issues and problematic behaviour is reprehensible in a lot of ways.

On the other hand, teachers are constrained by the same system children are. Teachers have to deal with thirty children in a classroom, standardized curricula they had no part in generating and frequent testing of their students by whose performance they are judged. Teachers of young children have to keep them inside for most of the day, have to maintain "curricular integrity," cope with a vast range of learning styles and needs and somehow keep a pack of young, active, energetic bodies docile and compliant all day every day. It is no small task, and one that requires immense patience and much technique.

In some respects I have a lot of sympathy for teachers working within an inane system and know the conditions they have to face. I do believe that most teachers want to work with children for good reasons, and the manipulative system they work within is not what they desire. I do believe that many teachers, given another set of conditions, could behave very differently. All that said, all teachers need to honestly assess their willingness to diagnose invented disorders and look for easy pharmaceutical answers.

It is with the larger system that primary responsibility should land, but all teachers would do well to consider their place within that system, if only in this regard. The unwillingness of institutions, and the people within them, to adapt to the vagaries of human biological variation is having spectacular consequences. As the institutional control of children becomes increasingly untenable, the attempts to control them pharmaceutically and / or psychologically are increasing proportionally.

There is also one other little note I want to add here. I acknowledge that many of these psychoactive drugs can be useful in extreme and crisis scenarios. I have had plenty of personal experience with youths whose conditions are severe enough that the use of drugs, sometimes even over extended periods, can be helpful. I am hardly an abolitionist about this. What I am against is the use of drugs as a social tool in support of schools. I think it is the institutional failings of schools that have given rise to the massive increases in pharmaceutical treatment, not any real need. It is schools and drugs in combination that is the problem, and the drugging of kids to avoid seeing schools in a saner light.

◎ ◎ ◎

There is a (sort of) funny story I often tell because I think it illuminates the thinking behind drugging school kids. Some time ago I came across a terrific headline in my morning paper: "Zoo polar bear put on Prozac to combat pacing."[102] Apparently the Calgary Zoo had a twenty-four-year-old polar bear named Snowball who had developed a habit of neurotically pacing back and forth across her area for up to 60 percent of her waking hours — a plainly obsessive and unhealthy pattern that was disturbing the zoo-viewing public. The zoo, in conjunction with a team of professionals, decided to treat the bear with Prozac as "therapy in a long-range plan for her neurotic behaviour."

The article quoted Dr. Bob Cooper, the zoo veterinarian, who offered that "maybe it's a psychological thing" and went on to point out that since the bear had begun the three-month treatment program, there had been a dramatic decrease in her pacing. To augment the approach the zoo was also using "environmental enrichment," such as hiding her food in chunks of ice, to help Snowball shake her malaise. There was also a team of researchers from the University of Calgary psychology department that monitored and videotaped the program, which according to the article is "believed to be one of the first major studies on the effects of Prozac on wild animals in captivity."

I realize the metaphor here is pretty obvious, but it strikes me as exactly the same crude logic that sees dosing little kids with Ritalin as acceptable. If you buy that the zoo is inevitable and the fact that

102. *Calgary Herald,* June 30, 1997.

the bear has to be there as a given, then giving Snowball Prozac is a logical next step. Viewed from a slightly different perspective, the whole project is one of cruelty and absurdity. It doesn't take a team of university psychologists to know that the bear is going nuts and the problem is not Snowball.

When speaking of a polar bear we are speaking of an amazingly active animal, one that roams for hundreds of miles, swimming, running and hunting. One can hardly conceive of an animal less suited to confinement. I don't think it's dogmatic hyperbole to suggest that Snowball's situation is analogous to schoolchildren's, though the bear is in more dire straits. In both circumstances it is the confined who is being forced to change, not the institution. I am deliberately trying to highlight the absurdity here, but it just isn't all that funny to kids who have spent big chunks of their youth in a pharmaceutical haze. There is a lot more to this story, and it is better told by those kids and families who have been directly affected. Ask around, you won't have to look far.

◎ ◎ ◎

There is one other piece I want to bring into this chapter. I am interested in the emergence of tools in our culture, and our understanding of their limits. The idea of technology is a recent one, emerging at the same time as "mechanical arts" or "industrial arts" began to converge into large-scale systems. The word reflected a new technocratic outlook, removed from toil, filth and noisy machinery, an emerging world view that has been poetically described as a "lack of sensuous specificity attached to the noun, 'technology', [a] bloodless generality."[103]

It wasn't until the late 1800s that the word "technology" began

---

103. Leo Marx, "The Idea of Technology and Postmodern Pessimism," in *Technology, Pessimism, and Postmodernism*, eds. Yaron Ezrahi *et al.* (Dordrecht: Kluwer Academic Publishers, 1994), 16.

to replace "mechanical arts" or "practical arts" as a description for the new tools and practices that were carried in by the Industrial Revolution. Leo Marx specifically ties the new term with the rise of both large complex systems and corporate America:

> During the nineteenth century, discrete artifacts or machines were replaced, as typical embodiments of the new power, by what would later come to be called "technological systems" ... Between 1870 and 1920 such large complex systems [for example, the steam engine and railways] became a dominant element in the American economy ... They included the telegraph and telephone network; the new chemical industry, electric light and power grids; and such linked mass-production-and-use systems as the automobile industry ... In the era when electrical and chemical power was being introduced and these huge systems were replacing discrete artifacts, simple tools or devices as the characteristic material form of the "mechanic arts," that term was also being replaced by a new conception: "technology."[104]

I think it is worthwhile to consider schools as a *technological system*, a conglomeration of disparate pieces and techniques tied to child-rearing, moving students as production units. More specifically, it is easy to see psychosocial learning drugs like Ritalin as a site-specific tool, a piece of a larger technology, and a logical extension of its mandate.

I am willing to hear an argument that there is a place in our lives for non-compulsory schools in limited and specific senses. I am also willing to hear that in some specific circumstances learning drugs might have a place and a real-use value. In combination, though, the two are nothing but trouble. When placed in the service of schooling, learning drugs lose all their value and become an absurd and harmful tendency.

104. *Ibid.*

Chris Mercogliano

Chris Mercogliano has been a teacher at the Albany Free School since 1973, and co-director since 1985. His essays, commentaries and reviews have appeared in many magazines, journals and collections, and he has spoken on numerous national radio shows. His first book about the Albany Free School, Making It Up As We Go Along, *was published in 1998 by Heinemann and his second,* Rid-a-Him, or Why are So Many Kids Labeled and Drugged in School?, *is published by Beacon Press. He is also co-editor of the internationally distributed quarterly* Journal for Living, *serves on the advisory board of the National Coalition of Alternative Community Schools and is a deacon in the Presbyterian Church.*

Mercogliano is a fine poet, carpenter, gardener and farmer. He is a former wrestler, quality baseball player and struggling basketballer.

I'm interested in the control of children in general, and in the context of schooling in particular. Talk to me about the emergence (historically or otherwise) of behavioural drugs as a school tactic. Did they start giving kids stuff in the sixties for hyperactivity?

Labelling kids preceded drugging them by a decade or more, with doping non-conforming students with biopsychiatric drugs a logical next step after assigning them medicalized labels like the currently popular "attention deficit hyperactivity disorder."

Widespread labelling was devised by the public school system in the 1960s as a defensive response when suddenly a whole new generation of suburban Johnnies was, for reasons unknown, slow to master the fine art of reading. Tried and true explanations like "cultural deprivation" had always worked fine in the past to explain why lower-class children had below-average reading scores in the primary grades, but such reasoning wasn't likely to go over very well with professional and middle-class parents.

One of the initial labels was "learning disabled," or LD. It adroitly explained away the alleged problem as one caused by a minor glitch in brain wiring. It established causation as physiological, not psychological, meaning there would be no need to examine whether home, school or other social influences might be contributing factors to a child's learning difficulties. Every schoolteacher and administrator knows that hell hath no fury like a parent made to feel guilty or at fault, so here was the perfect way out. And, perhaps best of all, such a simple, mechanical explanation left the door wide open for the application of a no-muss, no-fuss biomedical solution: medication.

Then every few years, one label morphed into another. LD became "hyperactivity," which later became "attention deficit disorder," which then became "attention deficit hyperactivity disorder."

Ritalin was first developed in the 1950s, but its widespread use didn't kick in until the seventies when it was heavily marketed as the best way to "treat" ADD.

What is the use of Ritalin like today? Is it the most prevalent school drug for kids?

According to the 1995 annual report of the International Narcotics Control Board (INCB), 10 to 12 percent of American boys were being prescribed the stimulant drug methylphenidate — more commonly known as Ritalin. The report also found that in certain school districts in Virginia as many as 20 percent of the male students were taking the drug. Meanwhile, the year 2000 INCB report reveals that the domestic manufacture of Ritalin increased over 800 percent during the previous decade.

In May 2000, a concerned deputy director of the Drug Enforcement Administration (DEA), Terrence Woodworth, testified before Congress that the use of Ritalin began to level off in 1999 and be replaced by even more potent stimulant drugs. Amphetamine sales in the United States rose over 2,000 percent during the 1990s, he reported. Woodworth's assessment was confirmed by IMS Health's *National Disease and Therapeutic Index*, a pharmaceutical industry intelligence publication, which announced in 1999 that the amphetamine blend Adderall — first marketed in the 1960s as a weight-loss drug — had overtaken Ritalin in overall market share.

Stimulants, while by far the most popular, are not the only drugs being used to control non-conforming children. More recently, antidepressants, antihypertensives, anticonvulsants, as well as various tranquilizers have been added to the mix, with many children being given multi-drug "cocktails" in order to produce round-the-clock effects. The actual number of young people currently taking one or more of what are now termed biopsychiatric drugs is difficult to determine, and estimates vary anywhere from six to over eight million American children. What we do know is that the figure continues to skyrocket, increasing 23 percent between 1995 and 1999, according to IMS Health. During this brief period the number of kids under the age of eighteen taking the antidepressant Prozac rose 74 percent; between the ages of seven and twelve, 151 percent; and under age six, 580 percent.

A study published in the February 2000 issue of the *Journal of the American Medical Association* revealed that the number of Ritalin prescriptions written for two- to four-year-olds went up nearly 300 percent between 1991 and 1995, with the total number of children in that age group receiving the drug estimated at 150,000 to 200,000. Meanwhile, a family practice physician in Syracuse, New York, recently informed me that the teaching hospital there is currently experimenting with Ritalin on *three-month-olds*.

What is Ritalin's effectiveness like in your experience?

If you give them enough, Ritalin makes kids eminently controllable in classroom situations. It dulls their impulses and reins in their attention like blinders on a racehorse. They will sit there and do boring, mindless activities right alongside the more passive and compliant kids. There are no studies, however, that show that Ritalin promotes actual learning. In fact there is one study indicating that long-term Ritalin use causes shrinkage of the brain by as much as 25 percent.

I have no personal experience with kids using Ritalin because we don't permit it. However, kids we get in our school who were taking it previously always report feeling much more at ease without it. Their headaches stop, appetite returns and growth resumes.

You have written about the degree to which Ritalin is prescribed overwhelmingly to boys. Do you think that boys suffer / react specifically in contemporary schools in ways that draw psychiatric / pharmaceutical attention?

Perhaps the most anomalous statistical aspect of ADHD is that the ratio of boys to girls who supposedly "have" it is generally recognized as at least four to one. Such a striking imbalance ought to arouse the curiosity of even the most nearsighted observer. A neurological disease that affects primarily one gender? It's a very unscientific notion.

Putting aside all the pseudoscientific gobbledegook upon which the purveyors of labels for non-conforming children base their claims, common sense tells us why the majority of kids being labelled would be boys. It is primarily excitement-seeking boys who are constantly frustrating the desire of teachers for smoothly running classrooms.

Let's face it; there are basic differences in the make-up of the young male and female psyches that have a significant bearing on who fits into school routine and who doesn't. A now-classic study of elementary-age school children conducted by the Fels Institute found that young girls learn primarily in response to the approval of their teachers. Boys, on the other hand, are motivated principally by the results of their own performance. Moreover, the approval of the other boys is far more important to them than the teacher's. I have observed this same phenomenon to hold true even in non-classroom contexts such as gymnastics, in which the activity the teacher is leading is one that suits the boys' basic natures and is something *they* want to be doing. So you can imagine how this fundamental difference in the learning styles of the two genders will play itself out in situations where the tasks are enforced and undesirable. It helps to explain why so many boys would be the ones climbing the walls in modern American classrooms, which have been stripped of almost all physicality.

A friend of mine recently suggested that girls have a kind of "psychic Ritalin" built into their systems. Girls, as the Fels study suggested, have a tendency to internalize automatically the control of the teacher — no need for chemical reinforcement here. Meanwhile, the dynamics of the conventional classroom, like the military or the modern corporation, require that students surrender their own wills, inclinations and internal rhythms.

The end result: increasing numbers of children, especially boys, who elect to challenge the system in the only way they know how, with aberrant behaviour and the refusal to pay attention, co-operate and perform.

All right, how about this argument: In a time of cultural fragmentation it is only strong institutions that bind our society together, and school, being the primary institutional site for children, has a special role in social cohesion. If kids are not compelled, by law or family, to attend, the culture begins to break down into individualism. Thus, if it takes

drugs or psychiatry to keep kids in school, well, that's unfortunate but socially necessary. Not only are these drugs administered for the kids' own good but for society's as well. Comments?

I have a slightly different take on the subject, one influenced heavily by Michel Foucault. In *Discipline and Punish* he discussed how societies throughout history have all had their ways of exercising power over people. However, a marked shift occurred from the mid-seventeenth century to the French Revolution, when emerging nation-states discovered the individual body as an object and target of control. Prior to this time, social control tended to take collective forms. Criminal punishment was carried out in large public forums; armies fought as a single mass; and what schools there were during the period functioned collectively, the students sitting at common tables rather than individual desks. Even knowledge itself was viewed more as a whole entity, rather than the compartmentalized set of separate fields that we consider it to be today.

The union of the new scientific paradigm and old forms of state power led to the development of individualized ways of controlling the activity, as well as the thinking, of every citizen within a given population. The aim of this nascent "disciplinary technology," to use Foucault's term, was to create a "docile body," one that may be "subjected, used, transformed and improved." Power began to evolve from the kind that directly oppresses people into subtler forms. For example, it came to be synonymous with individual productivity, which led to the drive for self-improvement and higher status. This meant that it gradually became unnecessary for society to use external power to control its members because citizens now kept themselves on socially acceptable pathways in order to reap the promise of future rewards.

The arrival of the nineteenth century brought increasing attention to the mass management of children. Prussia led the way by designing a national system of public education based on a combination of military and "scientific" princi-

ples. The openly stated purpose: enforcing orderly thinking
and behaviour among the entire nation's youth, as well as
inculcating them with notions of performance and individual
advancement. The Prussian system quickly became the envy
of Europe and the rapidly expanding United States, and
served as a template on both sides of the Atlantic. The
founders of the American public school system, such as
Horace Mann and others, spent two years in Prussia studying its school model so that they could copy it back home.

Today, the institution of modern schooling, through an
ever more exacting management of children's space, time
and activity, cranks out Foucault's "docile bodies" with
machine-like efficiency. For those children who resist, the
marriage of neuroscience and pharmacology has created the
means to extend society's reach *all the way to the biochemi-
cal level.*

Seen in the light of Foucault's analysis, biopsychiatric
drugs are control in a bottle. The drugs, along with their
accompanying labels, are a mechanical solution in the
mechanical system that the modern school has become. They
protect the assembly line efficiency of the classroom by bol-
stering the teacher's power to control a large number of students from a central location.

**Look, let's take this line seriously. If kids aren't in school,
where are they going to go? And they have to be kept there
somehow. In some ways that's what the thing is all about.
Parents gotta work, kids gotta go somewhere. That's all
there is to it. Have you ever tried to keep thirty kids in a
classroom all day?**

There's no question that the economy depends heavily on
the warehousing of children — the economical warehousing
of children I might add. And no, I haven't ever tried to keep
thirty kids in a classroom all day. Who would ever think of
doing such a thing?

Do you believe in learning disorders? Do you think that

ADD or hyperactivity or ADHD or dyslexia exist?

ADHD *et al.* — no way. There is absolutely no scientific evidence supporting the existence of a sudden epidemic of children suffering from an organic neurological disorder, whatever you choose to call it — a fact borne out by a November 1998 National Institute of Health (NIH) Consensus Development Conference on ADHD and Its Treatment. Consensus conferences are convened in order for experts to present scientific data about controversial medical issues to an independent panel or jury, which, after hearing all of the evidence, writes a final consensus statement. The statement is then handed out to the press, posted on the Internet and later published in a medical journal.

Even though, historically, NIH-funded research has overwhelmingly supported the labelling and drugging of children, and even though a decided majority of the experts selected to attend the conference had a pro-ADHD bias, the jury was forced to rule that the ADHD diagnosis remains speculative.

Meanwhile, I am willing to entertain the reality of something called "dyslexia" for three reasons: because it simply means "difficulty with reading," because so many so-called dyslexics report a similar experience of things like letters floating off the page and because drugs aren't generally seen as the "cure."

Entrusting Responsibility

A whole constellation of factors have conspired to leave perilously little room in kids' lives, and school and television are the primary culprits. It is not just actual time that is being so aggressively colonized though; it is physical space as well as the metaphorical space kids need to make themselves up in. A schooled culture just does not leave much room for enigmatic, unique development, and it requires a huge amount of bravery, courage and sheer moxie for a kid to imagine a non-standardized life.

The more I speak to people about schooling, the more it becomes evident just how widely schools are understood as technique-based. Invariably, when talking to people about alternatives, they will come around to, "Well, that sounds all fine and nice, but does it *work*?" This is a common question, and I think it an absurd one. Still, every year in almost every major city in North America, some organization, often a daily paper, will publish a survey of all the schools in the area, ranking them in order from best to worst. At one level it seems like simply holding the schools publicly responsible for their performance, but its implications are much greater than that. The project of identifying whether a school "works" assumes a set of standardized goals that can be objectively evaluated using outcome-based criteria, reducing child-rearing to a long series of assessable techniques. The logical next step is the training, professionalization and certification of those techniques.

Sometimes I get asked to check out a school or other program for kids, and often people ask me how I think the place is doing. It's an odd question, one that I can't answer. It's like going to a doctor for half an hour and asking "Am I healthy?" A doctor can give you a quick, subjective view: "You look healthy, your eyes seem clear, your energy seems good right now, your posture is fine, your weight is reasonable." A doctor can also give you some empirical data such as your blood pressure, cholesterol levels and respiratory capacity, and ensure that you don't have any obvious diseases. All of those factors, however, do not add up to "health."

Health is far more than that and might include, among many other things, stress levels, exercise, emotional stability, spirituality, relationships, eating, drinking, use of drugs and general outlook. Whether or not you are "healthy" is a question that only you and the people closest to you on an everyday basis could presume to begin answering.

Asking if a school is *working* (or presuming that they could be rated) is a strange question. No one would ask a parent "Is your parenting working?" or try to rate a neighbourhood of parents from best to worse. It would be a dumb question, and people would consider being rated as a parent extremely offensive. Parenting doesn't "work," unless there is an explicit, agreed-upon outcome, and mercifully few parents would be able to identify an objective "end" they wish for their children. Which is not to suggest that they aren't out there: there are certainly people who would consider their parenting a failure if their child didn't end up as a professional athlete.

Sure, most of us want our kids to be economically self-reliant and emotionally resilient, to find love and / or partners and all those standard things, but those are huge broad categories. "How is your kid doing?" is an immensely complex question that just can't be reduced to "What kind of grades is she getting?" Both we and our kids are much more than that. Taking the question of how your kid is doing seriously is a complicated proposition, full of answers that change constantly. Just like parenting, the business of good schools, or alternatives to school, has to be about what Dennison called the "lives of children."

I have heard a lot of homeschooling parents claim that the real reason they took their kids out of school is that the family just didn't have time to attend school and do all the things they wanted. It is incredible just how much time school consumes, between the six hours a day actually spent there, travelling to and fro, homework, preparations and then general decompression in the evenings and weekends, one could safely assume school eats a minimum of fifty hours a week. On top of school, add in the other dominating influence on contemporary children: television,[105] as well as videos, video games, extracurricular school activities and non-school classes, and then sleeping, eating and general care, and how much real time does a kid today have to create a life?

Aside even from the sheer lack of time contemporary kids have, we have entered an era in which children's ability to explore the world on their own terms has become increasingly constricted, largely under a rubric of "safety." Both in and out of schools, it has become acceptable to obsessively monitor and supervise children for their own good, and the idea of "safety first" has become cliché.

There is a great section in Daniel Greenberg's book about the Sudbury Valley School[106] where he describes trying to make their campus safe. The staff started getting concerned about the small stream and how far kids could play in it. They began to construct all kinds of rules around the stream. Then they started to look at the big rock and wonder how they should control children playing on it. Then the field with all its small holes started to look rife with potential threats to their kids' health. Then they realized that everywhere was a potential hazard; people find ways to hurt themselves in the most benign of circumstances, and it is only the kids who are genuinely able to keep themselves safe.

> We feel the only way children can become responsible persons is to *be* responsible for their own welfare, for their own education, and for their own destiny . . .
>
> As it turns out, the daily dangers are challenges to the children, to be met with patient determination, concentration, and most of all, care. People are naturally protective of their own welfare, not self-destructive. The real danger lies in placing a web of restrictions around people. The restrictions become

---

105. For a few contextual TV statistics, such as the hours per year the average U.S. youth spends in school (900) or watching TV (1,023), visit the TV Turnoff Network web site <www.tvturnoff.org>.
106. Daniel Greenberg, *Free At Last: The Sudbury Valley School* (Framingham, Mass.: SVS Press, 1973).

challenges in themselves, and breaking them becomes such a
high priority that even personal safety can be ignored . . .

Every child is free to go wherever they wish, whenever they
want. Ours is an open campus. Our fate is to worry.[107]

I think this is so right, and not just in the specific sense. We expect
kids to take good, responsible care of themselves, yet we still supervise them 24 / 7. We expect kids to be active, curious learners and
then keep them in a curriculum-driven school every day. We expect
kids to become good citizens or community members and yet insist
they live in undemocratic institutions for the bulk of their childhood. The way to develop responsibility, care, self-reliance, enthusiasm, curiosity, participation and self-discipline is to practise it,
live it.

> The most overwhelming reality of school is *control*. School
> controls the way you spend your time (what is life made of if
> not time?), how you behave, what you read and, to a large
> extent, what you think. In school you can't control your own
> life . . .
>
> What the educators apparently haven't realized yet is that
> experiential education is a double-edged sword. If you do
> something you learn it, then what you do, you learn. All the
> time you are in school you learn through experience how to
> live in a dictatorship. In school you shut your notebook when
> the bell rings. You do not speak unless granted permission.
> You are guilty until proven innocent, and who will prove you
> innocent? You are told what to do, think and say for six hours
> each day . . .
>
> The most constant and thorough thing students in school
> experience — and learn — is the antithesis of democracy.[108]

A schooled culture explicitly tells its youth that they are not to be

---

107. *Ibid.*, 109-11.
108. Llewellyn, *The Teenage Liberation Handbook*, 22.

trusted, that they cannot and should not make decisions for themselves, and kids learn to act as such from a very young age. People tend to live up, or down, to the expectations we have of them. When told that they are irresponsible and a danger to themselves and their futures, kids often behave like that. When they are trusted and given responsibility they invariably take it very seriously.

Parents and adults have to resist the impulse to laminate kids' lives. We have to let our children get out there, let them get their asses kicked once in a while and let them learn how to make real decisions about their lives. We have to trust that our kids want to take care of themselves and want to develop as much as we want them to.

I'm not arguing for letting your kids take crazy risks: letting your one-year-old charge into traffic or your four-year-old run around downtown by himself. It is kind of the opposite really. All too often kids ignore their own safety when they are accustomed to adults doing all the care for them, but they tend to be very careful of themselves when entrusted. The idea that kids need real freedom to develop is one that most adults sense instinctively; they understand what there is to negotiate. It requires being there *with* kids, being on their side, wanting their freedom — not shaping them to curricular expectations — and having a relationship with them. Kids don't want to damage themselves any more than anyone else does.

I acknowledge that this is a hard thing. Like Greenberg says, "Our fate is to worry." My children do not have anything like the liberty that I had as a child, and this is a pretty common experience, at least for those of us who live in the city. I was allowed to walk the couple of miles home from school at age six, yet I would never let my youngest daughter, Daisy, walk that far by herself now. At ten I packed a lunch into a canoe and paddled across the bay to swim and dive by myself. No way would I let my oldest, Sadie, do that by herself now. There are a lot of factors that go into these decisions, some of them right and good and some of them foolish and unreasonable. Trusting our kids to make good decisions is tough and it is something that, for me at least, needs constant consideration and attention. I know how I want to treat my kids; I just have to stay on it. This is also true in terms of getting kids out of school, and oftentimes it requires real discipline not to control our kids' days and make their decisions for them. It requires faith and trust not to revert, de facto or unconsciously, into reflexively schooling them.

It is part of a larger thing about trusting kids to make good decisions about their learning, their lives, their safety and their time: to take good care of themselves, in both the smaller and larger senses. In some ways this is exactly what most parents want for their kids, that they will learn how to take care of themselves and the people / places around them. Kids need time and room to become themselves, and that is never a simple or straightforward process. Kids, like all of us, need time away from school, away from TV, away from supervision, away from monitoring, testing and surveillance.

The wider political argument I am making has a lot to do with direct *participation*, and here I am pointing to a more personal rendition of the same control impulse. American planner and writer Sherry Arnstein has developed a Ladder of Participation[109] to describe eight levels of community involvement:

Citizen control

Delegated power

Partnership

Placation

Consultation

Informing

Therapy

Manipulation

I like this model plenty. It is meant for evaluating levels of citizen

109. Sherry Arnstein, "Ladder of Participation," in Ward, *Talking Houses*, 126.

participation in public planning decisions, like the creation of a new park or highway for example. The argument that Colin Ward makes in citing Arnstein is that in public planning we should always aim for the highest level on Arnstein's ladder: citizen control. I think it has a lot of value both for considering what goes on in schools, and for how kids get to make decisions about their lives in general — not just because it is good for kids but because it is a desirable way to live for all of us. British architect and builder John Turner has a lovely way of putting the exact same ideal, even though he is writing about houses:

> When dwellers control the major decisions and are free to make their own contribution to the design, construction or management of their housing, both the process and the environment produced stimulate individual and social well-being. When people have no control over, nor responsibility for, key decisions in the housing process, on the other hand, dwelling environments may instead become a barrier to personal fulfillment and a burden on the economy.[110]

A participatory culture requires social structures that are explicitly for the use of non-professionals: that is, everyday people who are not trained and not certified.[111] It explicitly suggests a local culture, community self-reliance and a decentralized control of resources and decision-making.

Deschooling and Social Ecology

I really want to be clear here, especially because I think this is where a lot of unschoolers run aground in their analysis. Standing

---

110. John F.C. Turner, *Housing By People* (London: Marion Boyars, 1976), 6.
111. This points to something that I once would have called *lifelong learning*. It was a decent idea now wiped out by corporate retrainers, computer colleges and parasites of all kinds driving working people into an endless cycle of retraining just to maintain the employment they already have.

against compulsory schooling has to mean standing *for* social change. Building alternatives to school cannot be just a different lifestyle, but must be an explicit argument for a different world. It is certainly true that much of the way we conceive of contemporary political and economic life is dependent on the way we conceive of schools, and the reverse is equally true.

To advocate a radical transformation of the school system is to advocate radical transformation of the social milieu that both creates and is created by schools. There are those who will argue that we can reform systems of schooling — maybe profoundly — and leave intact or perhaps even augment existing social, cultural and economic life. That's not me. I believe that there is simply a better way to bring up kids, and that there is a better way to live than consumption-based hypercapitalism. I don't think you have to be a social ecologist or an anarchist to agree with what I am saying about schools, but you have to know where I am sitting for this to make sense.

Over the last decade or so, activists across the globe have begun to name capitalist expansionism as *globalization,* a bold (historical, even) thrust for near-total economic and political control by corporate culture and state power. The attempt to loose capital from existing restrictions and create a one-world, 24 / 7 accessible market everywhere is the logic and language of a bureaucratized universalism gone berserk, and the only effective counter to that logic resides in popular community power.

The antithesis of globalization has to be local power, local control and local politics: municipalized economies, community governance and independent culture. We have to aggressively turn on institutions that are centralizing power and return control to local hands. To my mind there is no better place to start than state schools.

There have to be ways to make child-rearing a radically democratic project with community resources allocated by communities, and with families and kids in charge of their own days. We need to make growing up an actually *public* event, to make it far more public than what we call public schools now.[112] The project of making learning genuinely public is something like making democracies actually democratic. It has to be a radically decentralist project with two thrusts: 1) opposition, resistance and dissent, and 2) developing a fabric of community culture and institutions as a legitimate counter. The two thrusts have to work hand in hand.

Palestinian filmmaker Rashid Mashawari speaks of Palestinians not waiting to be given their self-determination, but going ahead and building their society:

> I don't want the American president or the Israeli president to give us a state because they can take it back at any time — I believe that the Palestinians should not wait for anybody to give them a state, that they should behave and believe that they are already a state. We've got problems — important problems. And we can spend the time (through art and culture especially) to build a society — and then it will be there.[113]

Now I doubt Mashawari would describe himself as a social ecologist or deschooler, but he elegantly expressed part of what I want to say here. This is how I can see the demise of state schooling coming about: not because some government gave away its power, but because of aggressive resistance — and because communities and families and kids grew something better. In endless combinations, alternatives to school are emerging simply because people are living better.

112. Describing state schools as *public* is emblematic of the confusion of our time and the contemporary malleability of words. It is a confusion that conveniently obscures real truths. Sure, schools are available to most everyone, mostly free of charge and created with tax money, but would you call prisons *public*? How about the military? These too are state institutions and do not meet the criteria of democratic control that *public* infers. Sure, school boards are elected, but democracy is reduced to lobbying and consultation, and elite interests invariably prevail.
113. Rashid Mashawari, speaking at a screening of his film *Live from Palestine* at the Blinding Light Cinema, Vancouver, B.C. (November 16, 2001).

Ⓞ Ⓞ Ⓞ

I place my analysis within the long tradition of anarchist thought, but am most engaged with social ecology as the best expression of that tradition. Social ecology is an expanding analysis that derives from the writing of Murray Bookchin and is rooted in his contention that the ecological crisis is not a result of overpopulation or industrialism per se, but is the inevitable result of hierarchy and domination: "ecology alone, firmly rooted in *social* criticism and a vision of *social* reconstruction, can provide us with the means for remaking society in a way that will benefit nature *and* humanity."[114]

Bookchin describes a "dialectical naturalism," echoing much of Peter Kropotkin, using the example of an endlessly diverse, self-organizing and mutualistic ecosystem as the best model for human society. He identifies the unique responsibility human beings bear for their ability to influence the natural world, emphasizing that ecological problems are at root social problems: that the domination of nature by humans is the *necessary* extension of the domination of humans by humans.

> The basic problems which pit society against nature emerge from *within* social development itself — not between society and nature. That is to say, the divisions between society and nature have their deepest roots in divisions within the social realm, namely deep-seated conflicts between human and human that are often obscured by our broad use of the word "humanity."[115]

Social ecology holds that capitalism, with its inherently hierarchical rationales, is fundamentally anti-ecological, and that when basic control and decision-making power are stripped from communities, the natural world is always the loser.

114. Murray Bookchin, *Remaking Society* (Montreal: Black Rose Books, 1989), 13.
115. *Ibid.*, 32.

Much of Bookchin's response draws heavily on the Greek *polis* and calls for a *libertarian municipalism*: participatory democracy at the local level, with decentralized democratic institutions organized within a municipalized economy. It would mean that "land and enterprises be placed increasingly in the custody of citizens in free assemblies and their deputies in confederal councils."[116] Bookchin takes the ideas of decentralized entities one step further and envisions them linked confederally, a community of communities, mimicking ecological interdependence.

The ideal of community self-reliance is hardly unique to social ecology, but it is so important because Bookchin hinges it on the dissolution of hierarchy, a larger ecological analysis, and a vision of social transformation. In the world we live in, it is difficult to contemplate such decentralization in the face of unrelenting urbanization and the paucity of actual cities; finding actual communities, let alone democratizing them, is a real problem.

It is here that I see deschooling as being so relevant to social ecology. Developing local democracies in a time of intense centralization of power has to start with counterinstitutions, that is, building living alternatives to social structures, and democratizing those that are worth revitalizing. Not only can counterinstitutions help us build the possibility and experience of local control, they can also form the basis for larger self-reliant communities. In that, I want unschoolers to see themselves as sitting right at the heart of real social change, not just personal accomplishment.

"Community" is one of the most butchered and misused words of our time, and its meaning has been almost entirely hollowed out. People take the word to mean a kind of ubiquitous good and use it

116. Murray Bookchin, "Libertarian Municipalism: An Overview" in *Green Perspectives* 24 (October 1991), 5.

to refer to almost any kind of social relationships now, from the business community to communities of women scholars to the community of wrestling fans. I knew the word was on life-support when in 1997 APEC[117] held its infamously protested international gathering in Vancouver and the posters promoted the event as "bringing the community together."

Despite all the hits and plasticizing the term has taken, the idea of community is still too important to let slip away. It has too much political significance for that. I do believe, however, that for the idea of community to hold on to value it has to mean a physical place. Community can't refer to networks or associations or gatherings of people (which is not to denigrate these affiliations).

Wendell Berry, through a long series of books, continues to articulate my favourite descriptions of community:

> By community, I mean the commonwealth and common interests, commonly understood, of people living together in a place and wishing to continue to do so. To put it another way, community is locally understood interdependence of local people, local culture, local economy and local nature.[118]

The local community must understand itself finally as a community of interest — a common dependence on a common life and a common ground. And because a community is, by definition, *placed*, its success cannot be divided from the success of its place, its natural settings and surroundings: its soils, forests, grasslands, plants and animals, water, light, air.[119]

In this, community can only be truly comprehended by those who live there and are committed to a particular place — local inhabitants who can identify the (usually shifting and permeable)

117. Asia-Pacific Economic Cooperation: an international trade organization composed of states around the Pacific Rim.
118. Wendell Berry, *Sex, Economy, Freedom and Community* (New York: Pantheon, 1992), 119-20.
119. Berry, *Home Economics*, 192.

boundaries. Even the best renditions of schools are not communities. They may be full of committed people, rooted in a neighbourhood and long lasting, but they are not communities in themselves.

Alternatives to school should view themselves as being at the heart of communities, as reflecting and creating the neighbourhoods around them, as permeable, democratic counterinstitutions explicitly about developing local power. Resistance to schools has to sit within an ideal of social freedom, not just individual autonomy.

Mary Leue

Mary Leue is a mother of five and grandmother of eleven. She has been a Maine farmer, registered nurse, teacher, civil rights and anti-war activist, lay midwife, leader in both alternative education and natural child-birth movements, therapist, community organizer, editor, writer, desktop publisher and bookseller.

In the 1950s she accompanied her husband to Texas where she raised her kids, taught schools and did graduate work in English literature and education. In the early sixties they moved to Albany, New York, where she began training with several internationally known therapists and doing graduate work in psychology. Leue started the Albany Free School in 1969, after her ten-year-old began responding badly to public school. Influenced by the ideas of Kropotkin, Gandhi, Reich and King, Mary believed that open, democratic education should be available to children of the poor as well as those of the middle and upper classes. When she consulted with A.S. Neill, he responded, "I would think myself daft to try." The school expanded to include a number of small-scale community institutions and continues to thrive. Leue now lives on family land in Massachusetts, produces two web sites and writes often.

So what are you doing these days?

Well, I'm definitely a farmer now. I've been living up here near Ashfield since early 1999. I heat the whole house with a wood stove in the kitchen, and in the winter I really only use two rooms, one upstairs and one down. And I have family, one son and his family on one side, and another son and his family on the other, all on the same property. It's 200 acres that I inherited. My mother and her lesbian lover bought it for $500 in 1909. Well, $500 for the first hundred acres and then $500 for another hundred acres with a spring on it that never ran dry.

I'm still running my on-line bookstore (Down To Earth) and I keep my two web sites going, Thoughts and Memories and Spinning Globe. I'm also on the council on aging in Ashfield, trying to get housing and medical facilities here in town, but so far no luck. Massachusetts is out of money, it seems. I work a lot on my web sites, which have different purposes, trying to give people some cues as to what it means to live creatively and with satisfaction in our society, especially in Spinning Globe, which focuses on schools. I'm eighty-two now, so with whatever lifetime I have left, I want to make sure that I put stuff that I think I've learned out there.

I want to ask you about community. It seems to me that the idea is one of the most misused and abused words of our time. Do you think the word still has value?

Sure, oh hell yes. It still has value. It's a very important concept, but lots of things they call community are really networks. People need to learn how to negotiate and compromise. In Albany we had established and developed ways of working things out. There's a Buddhist concept of community that includes the concept of an all-community meeting, of people hanging in there for resolution. Community will break down unless we practise it, which is what Scott Peck has said, unless you *do it*, it will vanish.

You can try to establish mini-communities, over distance, like on-line, but those are really groups, not really communities, pseudo-communities. I think you do have to have physical continuity for community to exist.

How can or should schools (or renditions of schools) support the development of community? What's their role? Where did you see the Albany Free School fitting into the neighbourhood?

Schools, or whatever sane version of schools we are talking about, have to be small schools, and they should be the *centre* of the community. In other words, it should not just be a place where trained people babysit kids. It should be a place and an institution that is used by everybody for getting together, for suppers and birthday parties and expeditions and so on and so forth. It should be semi-permeable to the community so that people, members of the community who want to come in and work with kids, and not just staff, are free to do that. And the reverse as well, kids who want to take on apprenticeships or work on projects with community members, that can be part of their chosen experience of growing up.

So in that sense there really should be no separate institution called the school, but school and community should be interactive, intermingling.

The AFS grew into the community in stages. After I bought the school building, I bought another building up the street at public auction (which became the Family Life Center), and I bought one four-storey building over on Wilbur Street for teachers coming in from other places that had no place to live. So staff could live rent-free, because we had no money. I did this using my mother's inheritance.

Then when we woke up to the fact that we needed some source of income, then we started using buildings for rental, and then using that money that came in to buy other buildings. The Free School now owns eleven buildings. It's like the title of Chris's book, we really did make it up as we went along.[120]

What's your general opinion about government funding and control of schooling?

Well, yes, the government has to be involved in some way, because there are many people and populations that just don't have access to the kinds of resources that I did, for example. The important thing is that governments don't try to control the schools, that schools maintain their autonomy, but I don't know how both things can happen.

Jerry Mintz says that the best free schools are those that were started by one person, or one couple or something like that. I think you could say the same thing about communities. And there have to be places for the coming together of small groups of people, and the opportunities, the resources have to be there for people to create physical spaces. The inner city is more amenable to these kinds of projects in some ways, because things are just so expensive in the country and the suburbs, sometimes less money has to change hands in poorer parts of the city.

I just don't know what the answer is. I think you are right that maybe part of the answer is to keep public funding very local. That makes sense.

There is a charter school halfway down the mountain here, between us and Northampton, and I know a guy on the board there, he used to come to my Live-Outs. I've visited there and they have done a pretty good job of keeping their autonomy and genuinely taking care of kids, but they don't have city kids because they are in a small community, and

---

120. See later section on independent democratic and free schools for the larger story of the Albany Free School, and also the earlier conversation with AFS director Chris Mercogliano, author of *Making It Up As We Go Along: The Story of the Albany Free School* (New York: Heinemann, 1998).

they tend to draw only middle-class families from Northampton. It's just fine and excellent as it is, but they don't have any poor city kids. There are a couple of inner-city charter schools in Massachusetts, there's one in Springfield I know, but I haven't had a chance to look at them yet. That is one example of a school receiving state funding and yet doing a pretty good job of staying autonomous.

I see there is some value to the charter school movement, but it's not something I have a lot of faith in. What I see there is the worst kind of compromise: government giving up responsibility while maintaining all the control. Charter schools still have to answer to the same people and the same standards.

That's right. The Free School never would have been accepted for charter funding. Never. You know Josh from Pathfinder . . . Northstar, that's what they call themselves now . . . he and Ken first had a charter school proposal for Amherst and they were turned down. And they are now thriving independently. It's very fortunate they weren't accepted, really.

I think you are right about how schools will be broken down, from a lot of different directions, giving in to pressure from so many places. It's kind of like the number of people who are running for different political offices as independents. I have never seen so many people running, and getting elected, who are not coming from one of the two parties. It has to be the way the political system is going to change, people rejecting the status quo.

We are living in a time of real transition, I think. Sometimes doing things independently, making fundamental changes, can have very negative side effects, but it is very necessary to do anyways. I think it is something like what we are going to have to go through with schools.

Do you think schools or alternatives to school or unschooling should be about producing good citizens or

community members? Because that really is what schools
and school people think they are doing.

Oh God, no! I know that's what schools think they're doing.
And the more power-hungry and imperialistic this country becomes, the more important that is to people. I come from a
very individualistic tradition here in Massachusetts.

No, they shouldn't be teaching citizenship or trying to turn
kids into citizens or community members. Not at all. Those
are outcomes. In a healthy institution for kids, where kids
are being treated the way they need to be treated, they are
allowed real freedom but are not abandoned just to their
own impulses.

If you are doing the right thing with kids, you are giving
them their space, but being there with them. Being yourself,
letting them be themselves.

In this kind of atmosphere they will learn how to be with
themselves and each other. They will learn how to be good
citizens, good community members. But that has to come
from within. You can't mandate that. You can't teach that.
You have to live that way. You know those books that talk
about how schools should be teaching emotional intelligence? What rubbish. That's not something you teach.
That's an interpersonal process. You can manifest it, person-
ify being a good community member, but you can't teach it.

4 The End of Compulsory Schooling

With a ringing laugh Pippi rode out through the gate so wildly that the pebbles whirled round the horse's hooves and the windowpanes rattled in the schoolhouse.[121]

How Things Are Changing

George Dennison opens *The Lives of Children* with this line: "There is no need to add to the criticism of our public schools. The critique is extensive and can hardly be improved on. The question now is what to do."[122] I think there is wisdom in this, which really doesn't explain why I just spent three-quarters of a book critiquing schools pretty comprehensively. Dennison wrote that in 1969, but what made schools so disabling then has only been exacerbated, and the questions about what to do remain.

When I'm feeling optimistic I can see a significant shift happening in North America. There is so much pressure, from so many angles, being put on monopolist state schooling that transformative changes cannot be too far down the line. This may be delu-

121. Lindgren, *Pippi Longstocking*, 61.
122. Dennison, *The Lives of Children*, 5.

sional on my part, but there is some evidence. The sheer numbers of homeschoolers, deschoolers and those enrolled in alternative, religious, independent and charter schools are creating an educational diversity that would make Plato weep like a baby.

The number of pedagogical and political challenges to compulsory schooling have multiplied, and those challenges that reach the highest levels are beginning to undermine the monopoly. It is widely accepted, even among the most ardent school supporters, that compulsory schooling in North America is approaching some kind of fundamental juncture, a critical mass of contradictions and discontinuities.

Arguments around school choice and change tend to break down into two distinct threads of discussion. One thread includes fundamental issues of state control and centralization of educational institutions — discussed extensively throughout this book. The other thread assumes that breaking down school monopolism is de facto a "good thing" in whatever form it comes. Within both threads, the conversation about how to structurally decentralize and diversify possibilities tends to be acrimonious and confused / confusing.

Much of a liberal centralist argument suggests that building institutional flexibility into school systems is all fine and good, but fundamentally the role of government is to maintain an equality of access to resources and services, balancing private interests within a greater public good. The corollary to this stance is that given an absence of state control of education, corporate interests would necessarily fill the void, and therefore undermining government monopoly is tantamount to handing schools and the children in them over to for-profit interests. The rest of this line of thinking then asserts that equality is an ideal that only government can protect, and that those opposed to state schools are in essence supporters of the kind of massive inequalities and injustices that privatization would bring.

This is the core philosophical underpinning to centralists' arguments about how school change can occur, and I think it specious and absurd. To suggest that an opposition to state control is to necessarily support corporate control is refusing to sincerely consider decentralist and / or community-based analyses. Reconstructive visions that municipalize or localize control over school resources offer the best solutions for realizing a deschooled society, and I think the process by which this kind of decentralization might occur is going to be asystematic, confusing and messy.

I have paraphrased Colin Ward a couple of times in this book already when I say that what we need is a mass of answers, not mass answers.[123] That is to say, I do not think that the school monopoly is going to be disassembled in an orderly, structured fashion, but by people building alternatives as viable and compelling counterinstitutions. It is wholly possible to reject centralized control in one form without necessarily reverting to it in another, though it is certainly a danger worth paying obvious attention to. In that regard, I think it is worth supporting every kind of alternative and charter school, every independent (even religious-based) institution, homeschooling effort, voucher proposal and deschooling group at some level because they all are putting pressure on the compulsory system. Whether or not I agree with their philosophical or pedagogical approach, I think it is worthwhile, at least in some specific respects, to support their efforts.

It is the control, money and resources that have to be municipalized for supporting as diverse a range of child-rearing scenarios as possible. In every community there has to be a fabric of schools and institutions emerging, very few of which any one person can or should support pedagogically. Necessarily all healthy communities do, and should, contain multitudes.[124] The point is to *politi-*

---

123. Ward, *Talking Houses,* 142. "There will be muddle and confusion, duplication of effort, wasted cash and misappropriation of funds. But what makes you think this hasn't happened in the days of big, public solutions?"
124. To paraphrase Walt Whitman.

cally support the existence of diverse institutional options while maintaining a radical critique of the *pedagogical* and *cultural* assumptions behind every effort.

This is not to suggest a retreat into a hollow relativism, but an insistence that decisions about what it means to grow up right have to be understood locally. The assumptions that a compulsory educative stance implies about social and class stratifications undermine conceptions of a common culture. It is not about providing any more middle-class options or more lifeboats for those who can afford them, but about creating the conditions for ethical child-rearing philosophies to flourish.

Change is going to come just as it is already coming: in pieces, often awkwardly, from all over and not really comprehensibly. That's good, but it doesn't mean that one should shy away from vigorous and forceful articulations of the kinds of places and relationships that are most healthy and compelling.

◎ ◎ ◎

I want to look at four threads of counterposition that I think hold the most promise for reconstruction: hijacking public schools, alternative schools and two separate alternatives *to* school: homeschooling and deschooling. Together these four form a rational and compelling resistance to compulsory schooling.

These categories are fluid, often blending into one another, and it is not important to make firm distinctions. For example, alternative schools will often accept homelearners part time, and homeschool resource centres may meet two days a week, making them look something like an independent school. Many kids would be happy to call themselves either homelearners or unschoolers. It is not the particular labels that matter, but the philosophical and political ideas at their core.

We can look to these four threads to see what is possible. Too often I hear people express dismay in the face of schools, as if the whole thing were just too daunting. Too often I talk to people who simply roll over and send their kids to the local school even though they hate it and their kids hate it. I hear too many families speak of loathing school as just part of our fate. I'm tired of it, frankly. Ever since the rise of compulsory schooling, people everywhere have been imagining and creating better lives for themselves. As Murray Bookchin has written, "The assumption that what currently exists must necessarily exist is the acid that corrodes all visionary thinking."[125]

I definitely know how huge the task of parenting is and that the lure of just sending kids off at age five and not worrying much about them during weekdays is a powerful one. I also know, very first-hand, just how hard it can be to find the energy, support, money and time to build real alternatives. But it is totally possible to create new institutions, to do things better, and there are examples everywhere to draw on.

Hijacking Public Schools

Behind this chapter lies a central programmatic question, one that is age-old and now cliché for activists: Is it worth trying to reform the system? My immediate reaction to this question, which I hear all the time, is no, not at all. And then my second reaction is, well, I don't know what the possibilities are like where you live, so maybe.

I don't think public schools are reformable. I think that they are too far gone, too far entrenched, too grasping to change much. As John Holt and Grace Llewellyn (respectively) have said:

> Do not waste your energy trying to reform all these schools.
> They cannot be reformed . . . You cannot have human liberty
> . . . if you give to some people the right to tell other people
> what they must learn or know.[126]

125. Bookchin, "The Meaning of Confederalism," 1.
126. Holt, *Instead of Education*, 6-9.

> I have no hope that the school system will change enough to make schools healthy places, until it makes school blatantly optional. But I have plenty of hope that people — you, your friends — can intelligently take greater control over their own lives.[127]

I tend to think that the "changing things from within" line is far too easy to drop and way too frequently invoked. That said, there are some excellent examples of public schools genuinely changing here in B.C.

I think that while the larger system itself cannot be reformed, individual schools can be radically reconfigured and, in certain districts, real innovation is sometimes possible. That is to say that public schools as a whole are not going to be taken over, but sometimes an individual school can be. It is certainly arguable that any work that good, smart people do within public schools is counterproductive in that it only props up a decrepit system and delays real change from happening. I generally support this line of argument to a certain degree, but then I think it becomes dogmatic. I have two kids who are part of a publicly funded, non-coercive school where I worked for many years and where my partner still works. It is a wonderful place in many ways, and my everyday experience renders arguing against the reformability of individual schools rather ironic, if not outright hypocritical.

For those interested in genuine change and finding innovative ways to work with youth, going through public schools is a pretty tenuous, but possible, proposition — especially in smaller districts where the bureaucratic weight is lighter and local officials are more approachable. I think that for someone to try to fundamentally change the nature of an individual public school, the circumstances and relationships have to be quite special. There are some good examples, though, of people taking over schools, either

127. Llewellyn, *The Teenage Liberation Handbook*, 16-17.

physically or pedagogically, and transforming them into something very different. In this section I want to look at two in particular.

The question still remains whether transforming a public school
contributes to a larger change movement. Perhaps it really does
just add legitimacy to a dying system, thereby inhibiting deeper
change, or maybe it is another direction to pressure the system
from, another method of slowly dissolving compulsory schools. I
don't think there is any way to answer that question definitively,
and it is possible both things are true, dependent on a lot of factors. Still, I think it well worth considering the examples of Windsor House and Lund in B.C., and chewing on the idea that they
may well be part of a larger answer.

◎ ◎ ◎

Lund is a small coastal community of about 800 people, just north
of Powell River. Like most small towns in B.C., the area is largely
resource-dependent, and it cannot be said to be thriving economically. It does, however, offer a great example of transforming a
public school.

In the late 1990s Lund's elementary school was in a serious
numbers crunch. The number of students (and thus available
school services) was declining precipitously, partially because there
were fewer kids around, and partially because many were com-
muting to Powell River or were homeschooling. In 1999, with
only five students enrolled, the school board decided to shut the
school down and received a sum of money from the provincial
Ministry of Education to assist with the transition.

A number of community parents, especially those with small
children not yet in school, were not happy about this situation.
They were determined that their children would go to school in
their community. A parent group began to organize and negotiate
with the school board to re-open the school as an alternative

school. In September 2000, after many negotiations, the board allowed the group to open the school doors as a distance education centre using a provincial curriculum. They were able to hire two facilitators to help the students, one for Grades 7 to 12 and one for kindergarten to Grade 6. This was the beginning of a journey of sorts for local parents.

The following year, for a variety of reasons, the school board pulled its funding. The parents scrambled, raised funds and hustled to keep the school running. They combined their efforts with a local community club, then proposed that the local government rent the school building from the school district and sublease it to this new amalgamated group, which would run not only education programs but community centre programs as well. They hired a certified teacher for the elementary program and continued to run the secondary program using the distance education curriculum, providing a tutor for help. The organization and financing of the school remained a real struggle, but the parent group hung in there with the major support of the Lund Community Society, whose backing provided much-needed organizational and financial support and community credibility.

In 2002–2003, the local school board agreed to fund the school again, but as a homeschooling centre, with the families using their own curriculum for the elementary program, and an Internet-based program for secondary students. The primary program now has a certified teacher in the classroom, and the secondary program is facilitated by a teacher's assistant. Currently there are eight children in the primary class and twelve students in the secondary program. It is called the Lund Discovery School and is hitting a groove, refining its curriculum and style, with classes Tuesday to Friday and students having the choice to work in the school or at home. The school draws heavily on the community for instructors and mentoring in a variety of fields, and the curriculum is built around what will work with the resources on hand. Evaluations are done by the facilitators in consultation with a school district teacher, especially appointed for homeschooling families.

It is a small story in some ways, but I think it's a great story. It shows what a group of families can do with a fraction of public school funding and just how capable local communities are of building their own alternatives. It also provides a living example of how schools can be physically taken over and remade to actually work. Ministries everywhere should be taking a hint here: close down the bureaucracies, tell the suits to go home, shut the schools, give the buildings to local parent groups and give them the money to work with. Then watch them flourish and you can claim it was your idea.

It's not that every little public school can just be taken over as such. There are all kinds of impediments, and Lund will surely face many more. On the other hand, it is clearly possible, especially if a critical mass of kids leaves. Schools rely on the agreement of their participants, and if that agreement falters, new circumstances are eminently possible.

◉ ◉ ◉

Windsor House, in North Vancouver, is another example of hijacking public schools. I have been involved with the place for about seven years now, and in many ways it's a unique institution. I don't really know of anything like it anywhere: a 200-student, publicly funded democratic free school for kids between the ages of five and seventeen that recently celebrated its thirtieth anniversary.

It got started in 1971 when Helen Hughes's daughter Meghan didn't want to go to school any more. One thing led to another, and soon Helen was running a small school with fifteen kids out of her North Vancouver home, and working nights to cover expenses. In time the school moved out of her house and into a long series of locations. The school eventually applied for funding from the school district, which, being a small jurisdiction in a more liberal time, approved it.

Since then the school has evolved in many different directions and gone through various incarnations. It has grown immensely and consistently throughout the past decade in terms of both staff and students. It has also seen its pedagogical and philosophical premises shift considerably, from a fairly conventional, liberal school structure to a genuinely democratic free school in the Summerhillian tradition (discussed next section).

The school has a staff of eleven, including teachers, aides and support workers, all of whom are paid as well as regular school board employees with full benefits. It is a parent-participation school and all families are expected to contribute two to four hours a week, either by working in the school directly or by helping with organization, cleaning or weekend work parties. The school has grown so big and so busy that parent participation is essential for running classes and activities, supervising rooms, cleaning and generally supporting the kids.

The facility is a terrific one: the top floor of a standard two-storey elementary school with a gymnasium and a full city block of grounds, including a huge blackberry patch, two small forested areas, playgrounds and a field.

For almost a decade now the school has been solidly engaged in refining and learning how to run a genuinely democratic, non-coercive school. The students are not required to take any classes or tests, do not get graded, do not receive report cards and are not pressured to participate in academic or any other activities they are not personally motivated to take on. There is, however, a tremendous range of classes and activities available, including all the standard classes plus field trips, hockey leagues, cooking and much more. Students are able to get credit for any grade they seek up to Grade 10. If students then want credit for Grades 11 and 12, they can enroll at another high school, work through a local learning centre, or graduate through distance education programs.

The school is run by democratic meetings and votes, although the nature of a public school is that many decisions are out-of-bounds. Within the range allowed, though, all decisions are up for all-school debate and vote, and everyone from the smallest five-year-old to the most senior staff member has the same right to speak and the same weight of vote. All rules are brought to a weekly resolutions meeting and voted on, and they are implemented by a judicial council run by a minimum of one staff member and five students. The judicial council, which has currently been folded into a larger school meeting, meets daily to discuss, debate and hand out consequences for violations. Any major disputes or issues can be brought by anyone before an all-school meeting, which has final decision-making authority.

In a lot of ways it is incredible that the school remains publicly funded, a feature that defines the inclusive character of the school. Parents pay between $10 and $60 a month, on a sliding scale, to an affiliated non-profit society that purchases supplies. Aside from that the school is entirely free for students, who come from all across the Lower Mainland.

There are some very significant drawbacks to the school's relationship with the school board, particularly around hiring. Windsor House staff can be hired only from a pool of certified teachers approved by the school board. The school district also exercises a significant amount of control over funding decisions, which in turn affect staff cutbacks, layoffs and hiring.

There are many other problems with the public-funding relationship, and all have to do with the board exercising power and control over every part of school life from safety requirements to enrollment to staffing to cleaning. There are, however, huge benefits, including free tuition and the resulting diverse student body, a well-paid and -supported staff, tremendous resources and huge financial support. These trade-offs are a constant struggle, but there is no question that Windsor House would never have been able to emerge and thrive as it has without the public money and support.

The reasons that the school has been able to maintain its funding are many and intertwined. Windsor House takes many students whom the district would have little idea what to do with otherwise. The school attracts scores of students — and their attached funding — from all over, bringing additional cash into the district. Helen has been ingenious at maintaining relationships, working within the system and with various administrators. The school has a large and occasionally aggressive parent body that has vigorously resisted past attempts to shut the school down. All these reasons combined, and many more flukes of circumstance and personality, have kept the school funding intact through the years.

There are real issues facing the school, and it is hardly perfect. The school is located in a suburb of Vancouver, which presents a real transportation challenge for many families, especially lower-income families who live downtown. The immediate neighbourhood is not especially supportive of the school, nor of its pedagogy, which often is a hassle. The school is not really connected with the larger community; it remains physically and pedagogically isolated and, though it is entirely open to parents, does not really serve as a community institution. But most of all, Windsor House's relationship with the school district will always be problematic, with the school always vulnerable to administrative agendas, pressure to conform, government cutbacks and schooled expectations.

Despite the pressures it faces, Windsor House manages to be a joyful and autonomous place for kids — unlike any other public school in this part of the world. As a new student once told me, "It's like I landed on the freaking moon."[128] That the school is not just existing but thriving is a testament to an immense amount of work, patience, vision and heart from a great number of kids, families, staff and, really more than anyone, Helen.

In some ways the conundrum of working within public schools is both essential and superfluous to any discussion of a saner world for kids. There is little question that the system of compulsory schooling is unsustainable. There is a tremendous amount of money and social structure supporting it, yet there is so much pressure and dissent from so many sides. It is inevitable that polit-

128. Myk Hodder, paraphrased.

ical, pedagogical and cultural change is going to swamp the schools we have now. The question is, what will replace them? It is important to me that people ask this question, not for some utopian future but for today.

Places like Lund and Windsor House demonstrate clearly that it is sometimes possible to work with what already exists, to fill vacated space either physically or pedagogically. The driving forces for real change necessarily have to come from outside the system, but sometimes schools can be taken over and retrofitted. Such projects exert a vision that's important not just for the present, but for the long term as well.

Independent Democratic and Free Schools

There have been independent schools more or less forever, and before the rise of government schooling they were the norm. For the last 150 years, however, in the face of compulsory state schooling, independent schools have come to mean something necessarily counterposed to public schools. Prior to monopoly schooling, independent schools could exist, attract students and represent themselves pedagogically and philosophically as a "good" in and of themselves. Now, though, independent ventures are by definition "alternatives"; that is, they have to justify their existences in terms of their difference from the dominant norm.

In the context of conscious alternatives, there have always been independent projects swimming against the tide of public schools for every reason imaginable. The most common type of independent school has been and will probably always be religion-based. Ideals of religious freedom remain sacrosanct in most parts of the world, and as such the existence of religious schools has long been acceptable, even to the most ardent of state school advocates.

As soon as state schools were established and it became obvious how they were going to operate pretty much everywhere, opposition developed. The bureaucratization of learning, the standardized curriculum, the abstraction of data, the positivist tendencies, the testing, the rote memorization, the rewards and punishments and all the rest drew swift and lasting pedagogical and political responses. Since the early decades of the twentieth century, when public schooling took on its present shape and substance, alternative secular schools have proliferated. These various alternative schools, some of which have grown into movements, have never become so popular as to threaten the hegemony of public schools, but they continue to flourish in virtually every community in North America.

Many of these schools are based on the research, writing and / or personality of a single person, such as Montessori, Steiner, Pestalozzi, Carden and Comer. Through practice, introspection or spirituality, an educator may believe he or she has found a better way to learn, a better way to organize children and a better way to run a school. Many of these schools rise and fall quickly, usually with their founder, but some create greater resonances and take on larger trajectories. Today Montessori and Waldorf (Steiner) schools, for example, have become international movements with thousands of schools across the globe and can be found in almost every corner of North America.

Personally, I'm leery of any school based fundamentally on the writing or thinking of a single person. I am suspicious of those educational gurus who believe they have unlocked the secrets of how kids learn best. I simply don't buy it. The complexity of individuals can be represented by their learning styles and patterns, and how any one person learns best is an ever-shifting stew of circumstance, personality, relationships and much more. For anyone to attempt to describe how kids learn, or to generate models or systems for educating children in general, seems absurdly arrogant and futile at best. Figuring out how the kids right in front of you can flourish and what it means for them to grow up well can only be done in the context of place, relationship and time.

It is important to make clear, however, that in spite of my philosophical objections to certain kinds of schools, I support the existence of them. I want to see a vast array of independent schools flourishing in every community, whether or not I like what they are doing or think them valuable or compelling. Breaking down monopoly schooling means just that; in a better world, independent schools of almost every kind will have the chance to emerge.

◎ ◎ ◎

The trick to independent schools, of course, is funding. Religious schools, most notably Catholic schools in this part of the world, have always flourished because of the tremendous fiscal resources of many churches and religious bodies. Without major financial backing from the church or state, independent schools have to scramble to find the money to operate. Religious schools in North America have consistently broken legislative and political ground for independent school funding and acceptance, and secular schools have tended to follow in their wake. The trouble is that non-religious schools infrequently have deep financial resources and so tend to emerge as middle- and upper-class options, driven by tuition and parental support. Independent schools that want to be something more than that are always challenged by money.

I have been there. I am there now. I know how hard it is to run an independent project, especially in a poor neighbourhood working with lower-income kids and families with little outside support. It is very tough to run a truly independent place, and so many alternative schools have become middle-class enclaves because they are forced into becoming tuition-driven. I firmly believe that alternative schools and projects *must* be something more than middle- or upper-class refuges or else they become regressive, not progressive projects. A vision of social change has to be present and articulated.

I have heard the argument over and over from good people that their schools are great places, that they deserve to exist and the only way they can survive is by catering to families who can pay hundreds of dollars in tuition each month. I understand the logic, but I do not think it defensible, not even for wonderful and amazing schools, including some in the democratic tradition, schools that have incredible faculty, beautiful campuses and fantastic histories. All independent schools and projects have to be something more than another middle-class option. They have to be conceived as open to all kids and families, especially to poor and marginalized communities. Good people and good places, if they are working to benefit only the children of the most privileged class of people in world history, are of dubious value.

In that light, a vision of disassembling compulsory schooling relies on independent schools finding the resources, support and innovation to be able to thrive in disparate communities. Whether or not answers lie with alternative schools receiving public funds, sane versions of educational credits or vouchers, public granting, or however else an equitable resource distribution can be conceived, they need to have equal access to what resources and support exist. The funding already resides in each municipality, but is squandered needlessly on compulsory bureaucratic schooling. The money is already there and being spent in the name of kids; it just has to move pockets.

In a better time there will be waves of independent schools everywhere; it will be easy to start them, in micro renditions, in houses and basements and offices; and the regulation and funding that is now geared to support state schools in every possible way will be reconceived to encourage small schools and projects everywhere.

◎ ◎ ◎

I want to look at a specific vision of alternative schools. I want to talk about *democratic* and *free schools*, which are separate things,[129] but I am most interested in schools that attempt to be both. I want to be clear on this: it is absolutely true that kids and families have to be able to create or find educational opportunities that reflect and support their vision of the good life. Communities have to be willing to support disparate visions, ideals that look nothing like one another *and* that do not preclude vigorous discourse and critique about the nature and style and content of those places.

I want to speak of the democratic free school tradition because I frankly think it is a compelling and important articulation of adults and kids living together well. I want to briefly highlight three separate schools: Summerhill in England, the Albany Free School in upstate New York, and a little learning centre called Eastside Wondertree (I know it was a dumb name: long story) that my partner, Selena Couture, and I ran here in East Vancouver. There are many more that are worth looking at, like George Dennison's First Street School in New York City or Tokyo Shure in Japan, but I chose these three to demonstrate a range of constructions and to make a point about building a fabric of alternatives.

There is no guru of the democratic school movement nor any place to point to as a beginning. It is not A.S. Neill nor Tolstoy nor Ferrer nor Lane nor Rousseau nor Holt who is the wellspring. All these folks, and many, many more, have drawn on the same river of ideas, a long flow that I think is best named anarchist or libertarian, and directly democratic. Respecting the choices of children,

---

129. Free schools are *non-coercive,* that is they do not have required classes, and students are free to determine how they spend their days. Democratic schools are those that have mechanisms for all students and staff to participate in the organization and regulation of the school. Some schools are one or the other, but most free schools attempt to be democratic, while the reverse is not always true.

self-government and non-compulsory learning are ideals that have no taproot but have existed in various forms forever.

For this chapter, though, considering independent schools that are necessarily counterposed to state schooling, the best place to pick up the thread is with Summerhill.[130] Drawing on Rousseau and Tolstoy, and more specifically on Homer Lane's Little Commonwealth[131] and the developing psychoanalytic approaches of Freud and Reich, Neill founded a school in the 1920s on two essential principles: self-governing school meetings and the primary importance of children's emotional well-being. His daughter Zoe Readhead (now the head of the school) says that

> Summerhill has not changed fundamentally since it was first started. Its aims could be described as the following:
> - To allow children freedom to grow emotionally;
> - To give children power over their own lives;
> - To give children the time to develop naturally;
> - To create a happier childhood by removing fear and coercion by adults.
> Allowing children freedom helps to develop self-motivation. Emotionally healthy children are not inhibited in their learning process. Giving children power over their own lives promotes a feeling of self-worth and of responsibility to others. They learn from an early age what they think is important and that others will listen to what they have to say.[132]

Summerhill has always been a boarding school, with around half its students (now approximately eighty kids) coming from out of

130. See A.S. Neill, *Summerhill: A Radical Approach to Child Rearing* (New York: Hart, 1960) or *Freedom Not Licence* (New York: Hart, 1966).
131. E.T. Bazeley, *Homer Lane and the Little Commonwealth* (New York: Schocken, 1969). This was a 1910s experiment in which Lane took "delinquent" teens to an isolated rural property and developed a scheme for self-government and direct democracy.
132. Zoe Readhead, "Summerhill School," in *Deschooling Our Lives*, ed. Matt Hern, 110.

country, many from Japan. That the school is self-governing means that almost all decisions about daily life are made by democratic process with all community members having the same vote. One of Neill's signature lines was "Freedom not licence," meaning that the freedom experienced at Summerhill is a social freedom, that is, one does not have a licence to "do as one likes." Within that freedom there are many rules, ongoing debate and discussion about everything from bedtimes to the use of bikes to class times.

Neill's book *Summerhill* arrived in the United States in 1961 and had a tremendous impact, such that by the mid-seventies there were more than 1,100 free schools operating in the U.S. Since that high tide the numbers have fallen off significantly and there are far fewer currently alive in America. The numbers are sometimes hard to pin down as many little free schools are constantly springing up and an equal number fading away or transforming themselves. For example, many people who once would have called their places free schools now call them homeschool resource centres. As Jerry Mintz explains in the following section, it is not so much that the free school movement went away, but that it has been reconstituted in different forms. The influence of free-school thinking remains evident in many public school reforms, in kids' camps and drop-in centres and youth projects around the continent, and especially in the development of homeschooling and unschooling movements.

The energy and vision of free schools in the late sixties and seventies has not sustained itself into a new millennium, but a democratic school movement certainly exists and is thriving in many ways. One of the best is the oldest American inner-city free school in Albany, New York.[133] The Albany Free School (AFS) was founded in 1969 by Mary Leue when, as with so many other alternative schools, her school-age son needed a better place to be. Gathering a few other kids around her, Leue opened a school in a

133. For a better, more complete history, see Chris Mercogliano, *Making It Up As We Go Along.*

poor downtown neighbourhood and, wanting it to be fully integrated, challenged middle-class whites to leave their uptown
enclaves. Locating themselves within the burgeoning free-school
movement, the school adopted many Summerhillian approaches,
among them school council meetings for decision-making on the
premise that only those who were actually present in the building
day to day should determine policy.

One of its best aspects, and a real key to its longevity, is the Free
School's financial vision. Leue understood that if the school was
simply tuition-driven it would be almost impossible to escape a
middle-class trap. Early on, with a small inheritance, they started
buying up cheap abandoned buildings on the same block as the
school and renovating them for teacher housing and rental
income. Now the school owns ten buildings in the compact neighbourhood, providing an essential financial base to work from. The
school still charges tuition, but it is on a sliding scale that can slide
all the way to nothing, and no one has ever been turned away for
financial reasons.

That larger community vision has kept the AFS both vital and
flourishing through the years when so many other places have
faded. Many of the Free School teachers themselves began buying
up cheap houses in the neighbourhood and fixing them together,
then expanding into developing community institutions. Over the
years they have started a Family Life Center, providing midwifery
services and childbirth and pregnancy support; a small natural
foods store; a book and crafts store; and they now own two country properties for camping, excursions and workshops.

So much of the Free School's success is rooted in its place. The life
of the neighbourhood is the life of the school, something that you
can't miss when visiting. It has the feel of an intentional community, but without the escapism and lack of social engagement. It is a
group of people committed to conscious living, with a small school
at its heart, and the democratic principles of the school are integral
to its wider vision. It's the willingness to work with kids and people
from where they are that I like so much, and the paucity of dogmatic

arrogance. As Chris Mercogliano wrote once, "There is little in the way of a long-range plan. We will continue to trust in God (but tie our camels!), and let one step lead us to the next."[134]

⊙ ⊙ ⊙

When Selena and I opened our little school we had a lot of the Albany Free School in mind, as much as we had anything in mind. Over the years I have heard many folks say that they "didn't know what they were doing," but my goodness, we *really* had no clue.

To make a long story short, we were very young, had just arrived in Vancouver from New York City, had virtually no money or jobs, but did have a young baby. After a little messing around we located a group that was closing an independent school after ten years of operation and was offering to assist new schools in forming. It was an important relationship because, for a variety of complex bureaucratic reasons, it allowed us to access public funding right from the start. Independent schools in B.C. are required to have been in operation for one full year before they can apply for funding, the maximum level of support being half of what public schools are allocated, or at that time approximately $2,800 per kid per year. By affiliating ourselves with an already functioning (and funded) school we were able to slide past that one-year probationary period.

Our project stayed alive through more than four turbulent years, eventually closing in 1995 when our emotional and financial resources finally ran dry. In retrospect it amazes me that we thrived for that long. In the end it was the City of Vancouver that really got us. By leaps and bounds our biggest challenge throughout the entire thing was dealing with city zoning and building departments. The absurdly Kafkaesque requirements of running a small school in the city were made apparent to us through hun-

134. Chris Mercogliano, "A History of the Albany Free School and Community," *Deschooling Our Lives* , ed. Matt Hern, 119.

dreds of hours of negotiating, lying, posturing and pleading with various offices, almost always with limited success.

We were willing to run the school almost anywhere. The last two years, which were great, we operated out of a cavernous, old concrete-block warehouse with almost no heat. It was indestructibly perfect. Then, forced to move from that location, we spent a frantic summer hunting, eventually settling on a second-floor industrial space that all relevant city officials approved until one final fire inspector had a last look and ordered upgrades that would cost $38,000, including two whole new firewalls, increasing the width of each step by three-quarters of an inch, and partial sprinkling. It was enough to finish us.

Strangely, finding a suitable building has always been the biggest problem for independent schools, as Jonathan Kozol wrote thirty years ago:

> Incredible building codes, obtuse bureaucracies and openly inconsistent supervisors seem to be one of the constants in the ritual of North American oppression. The building code, so blatantly and often tragically ignored in cases of old, collapsing, rat-infested tenement houses owned by landlords who have friends within the city's legal apparatus, are viciously and selectively enforced to try to keep the Free School people out of business . . .
>
> In Boston, it is easier to start a whorehouse, a liquor store, a pornography shop or a bookie joint than it is to start a little place to work with children.[135]

What Kozol says is consistently true: in far too many cities it is ridiculously hard to find a little place to work with children. Eight years down the road, I don't feel resentful that it was our building that did us in, but I do feel like we had something going for a while. We were working in our neighbourhood of Commercial

135. Kozol, *Free Schools*, 27-28.

Drive on the east side of the city, where we still live, with a poor and scrappy group of parents, trying to figure out some combination of a free school and community learning centre. We were able to survive with a low tuition that slid relentlessly and frequently, we worked with a great bunch of kids, many of whom we are still friends with, and we ran a terrific project.

We deliberately stayed small, with between ten and twenty students. Selena and I worked half time each and took care of our daughter, Sadie, half time, although there was a lot of overlap and as Sadie got older she spent more and more time at the centre. Our pedagogy was fluid and we were willing to try almost anything. We travelled and camped, went out to the country once a week, brought in community art and music mentors, cooked and ate together, made various runs at sustained academic work and generally tried to always be *doing* things, together and individually. We were never "democratic" in the school meeting / voting / Robert's Rules sense. Whenever there was a decision to be made we sat around the big table and made it together. It was sort of consensus, though we never followed any "process" (aside from letting everyone have their turn with not too much interrupting), and it was "democratic" in that everyone contributed equally. We never voted formally, unless it seemed really necessary, and I can hardly remember that happening. Our explicit intention was respect and equality and everyone getting what they wanted. The closest thing to describe it was *family*.

In many ways we looked like a free school, and we were at our best when we didn't try to be like a school at all. We were most successful when we challenged ourselves with the biggest questions and didn't try to achieve schooled ends by nicer means. We didn't follow any model, and answered really only to the kids and parents, and to our broadest ideals.

I think there are at least nine key characteristics of democratic free schools:

- Non-compulsory academics

- Democratic self-government — school meetings hold the power
- Self-regulation — faith in the ability of children to make good choices from a very early age
  - Non-graded evaluations
  - Non-compulsory attendance
  - Focus on emotional / social development over academic
  - Non-hierarchy of activities
  - Broad interpretations of learning
  - Importance of play

Most or all of these aspects are true of democratic free schools, and most were accurate descriptions of ours. Selena and I were at our best, though, when we took these ideals not as prescriptions but as raw materials to work with, and I think that is true of all the free schools I have visited. Schools become bogged down in dogmatism and self-referentiality when they try to adhere to a program or model. It is the ideas that matter most, and trying not to bureaucratize their expression.

Democratic free schools aren't for everyone, to be sure, but they represent a body of theory, knowledge and experience that may form the most important living alternative to state school pedagogy. If compulsory schooling is to be disassembled, there is little question that democratic schools have to be a real part of that. That said, there are also trenchant critiques that should be equally considered.

In a lot of ways the democratic school tradition is reviving itself in the twenty-first century. The wave of conservative educational praxis that was energized in part by the Reagan administration, William Bennett, Allan Bloom and the rest has chilled somewhat and many new schools have sprung up all over the world. New incarnations rarely call themselves "free schools" for fear of evoking too many hippie-dippie apprehensions, preferring the more innocuous "non-coercive" or simply "democratic," but it is the libertarian Summerhillian tradition many are clearly working with.

Many of the easiest critiques of free schools focus specifically on their apparent lack of structure and loose attitudes towards discipline. It is certainly true that almost all free schools are vastly wilder than traditional schools. The noise is often excessive, and sometimes there is a lot of random, wild energy. It is often hard to find quiet-enough space to focus. The order that emerges can seem closer to chaos, especially for sensitive adults with constructed ideas about what kids should be doing with their time.

These observations are all largely true, but strike me mostly as a matter of individual preference and style. Some people like the looser, louder feel of free schools, others do not. Some kids thrive in democratic schools right away, some kids can't stand the atmosphere. The important critiques, though, are directed more at whether or not these schools are a "good thing," and less at whether or not they "work." The point of these critiques is to determine whether or not they are a realistic part of a new vision.

The most incisive critiques of democratic schools are tied up with core knowledge proposals. In non-coercive schools, kids are given the freedom to pursue those activities that most interest them, which means most do not engage with anything like a common curriculum. It is an individualist ethic, one that can tend to atomistic intellectual development, with each child's skills and knowledge having little relation to those of the others around her. Non-coercive academics means that very few kids end up studying anything like a canon, even loosely constructed.

I have already spent considerable time assessing the imposition of a canon, but I do think there is some merit in this argument. I wonder and worry about kids who grow up only studying that which interests them, and have real concerns about the lack of cohesive intellectual enquiry that happens at the free schools I have known. It is not that excellent, complex and comprehensive academic work doesn't happen in radical schools. It does, and I believe from years of first-hand experience that kids learn far better and deeper when they are engaged in studying something they are genuinely interested in. I also believe that in a non-coercive context it is possible to genuinely address what it is important to know in a *community context*. At the same time, I really wish that free schools were more aggressive about defining that.

Maybe even more important is the critique of "natural development," an idea that democratic free schools tend to mouth. Non-coercive academic theory suggests that children will engage intellectual challenges — like reading, regular classes, math, getting into post-secondary education — "when they are ready" and that kids should spend their time doing that which interests them. These are ideas I agree with, and yet in the absence of competing activities, what tends to rush in for kids is dominant culture. The culture around them is an aggressive one that actively places demands on kids' lives and actively tries to shape them. Too often free schools do too little to pose themselves as counterforces, interpreting freedom as non-interference, and nurturing an individualist ethic that tends to support selfishness.

I think this critique a salient one that stems from many free schools' apolitical sensibility. Working with kids is inherently political, and allowing children to develop "naturally" cannot mean churning out happy, selfish people. Giving kids the opportunity to learn what they love is great, and it has to happen in the context of relationship and community. Just as "freedom not licence" implies a social freedom, what people do with their time has to be a social question. Too many democratic schools allow a non-coercive pedagogy to overwhelm ideals of social change, community and political living.

For me, after working with free schools for all of my adult life, the most cutting of critiques runs along Illichian lines. Ivan Illich's analysis of disabling or manipulative institutions is that they are social structures that undermine people's ability to run their own lives.

> Many students, especially those who are poor, intuitively know what the schools do for them. They school them to confuse process and substance. Once these become blurred, a

new logic is assumed: the more treatment there is, the better are the results; or, escalation leads to success . . .

The free-school movement entices unconventional educators, but ultimately does so in support of the conventional ideology of schooling.[136]

It is arguable that free schools in some ways replicate the disabling capacities of schooling per se. That is, they do not fundamentally posit themselves as tools, but in fact become institutions that their students need to thrive, places that students come to believe are essential for their "education." In this way free schools maintain the same hold traditional schools have over their students, instilling in them the deep belief that it is only through the institution that a better, more competent life can be achieved. In this view, free schools are a nicer form of school to be sure, but hardly liberating. It is a complex and worthy argument, one that I return to often, and one that I will look at further.

That many of these critiques have real resonance, and there are others, is readily acknowledged by those most deeply involved in democratic free schools. They are not simple or easy challenges, but they can provide both the physical and pedagogical space to engage fundamental questions about childhood. These schools are not perfect, they're not for everybody, there may be endemic issues about their intent, but there is a core of very compelling praxis.

In the end, I would like it if there were democratic free schools everywhere. I frankly have a lot of faith in the tradition. They do not suit every child or family, but they do represent a real and important part of getting out from under the rock of compulsory schooling. I think that free schools speak to a way to live in the world with respect and care for children, especially if they are conceived as much more than schools, and as institutionally fluid.

136. Illich, *Deschooling Society*, 1, 80, 95.

Jerry Mintz

Jerry Mintz has been a leading voice in the alternative school movement for over thirty years. He worked as a public school teacher and a public and independent alternative school principal for seventeen years. He founded several alternative schools and organizations and became the first executive director of the National Coalition of Alternative Community Schools, serving from 1985-89. In 1989 he founded the Alternative Education Resource Organization, which he continues to direct, and is editor of its networking magazine, The Education Revolution. *He has lectured and consulted with schools and organizations in the United States and around the world, including Russia, the Czech Republic, France, England, Israel, Denmark, Holland, Ukraine, Japan and Austria. He has published hundreds of articles and studies on educational alternatives and was editor-in-chief for the* Handbook of Alternative Education, *which lists 7,300 educational alternatives.*

So what is a democratic school? Are they all like Summerhill? Are people averse to calling themselves free schools for fear of sounding like hippies?

The easiest way to answer that is a democratic school can be a free school, but not necessarily. A school can

practise democratic procedures but still be coercive. There
are a few places left that I know of that still call themselves
free schools: Albany, New Orleans and Grassroots Free
School in Tallahassee, Florida. But yeah, I think the name
just sounds anachronistic to people these days, and also there
is a little confusion as to whether you had freedom there or it
was free to go, as in "didn't cost anything."

There are many schools around the world that call themselves democratic, and those schools, generally speaking, are
specifically democratic in that the students are actually
empowered to make decisions about the school and their
own education. And not all of them, but a percentage of
them, are not only democratic but non-coercive, meaning
that the kids are not required to go to classes. A Summerhillian school would have those two aspects. And there are
lots of schools that have one aspect or the other, but not
both.

**Would you say there has been a revival of the democratic
school movement? How many are out there?**

That is a matter of definition. We have 12,000 educational
alternatives in our database. And that covers a whole spectrum. How many schools consider themselves to be democratic? I'm not sure. I would say that there may be five
hundred. It is hard to estimate how many free schools are
out there because there are many that are not connected to
any network, and so we may not know about them. A lot of
the new small places that are starting, particularly homeschool resource centres, are very often non-coercive, and one
of the reasons they can stay non-coercive is because techni-
cally the kids are homeschooling, so they're not required to
force their kids to go to classes. Then you see this whole gra-
dation: is it a homeschool resource centre if it only meets
once a week? Twice a week? You know what I mean?

In a lot of ways things have morphed in different directions. But I would definitely not say that the phenomenon
has ebbed. That is, it has changed, but I think it was a myth

that the free-school movement or the alternative school movement ended at any point. What happened is that it tended to go underground, especially during the eighties, and there is still a strong tendency among surviving schools to be low-profile. But for example, the alternative education movement gave rise to the homeschool movement. And there are now two million people homeschooling. A not insignificant number, and that's just in the United States. And it also gave birth to the charter school movement. There are many kinds of charter schools, but the impetus behind them is to get out of the regular system. The first charter school started in 1991 and now, eleven years later, there are 2,700 of them.

I think the commonality of this movement is to have a learner-centred, more individualized approach, rather than a curriculum-driven approach.

I do think that there has been a revival specifically of democratic approaches though, and as time goes on I think it is only going to continue to expand. In Russia, for example, there is a democratic school called the School of Self-Determination that, among other things, has non-compulsory class attendance. It is a public, inner-city school with 1,200 kids. And, last I have heard, they have seventeen other democratic schools that are part of that network. Then you go just a little beyond that, to the Eureka network, also in Russia, and they have about 650 schools. And you go a little beyond that, and we introduced the idea of Montessori at a conference I went to in 1991, the first New School Festival of the Soviet Union (a week later there was no Soviet Union), and now there are over a thousand of those schools! We discovered that at the tenth anniversary conference of the first New School Festival, which I attended in Moscow in the summer of 2001. They now have a biweekly alternative education newspaper there with a circulation of 250,000.

So this is a worldwide thing. In England there are possibly 100,000 homeschoolers now. There are cracks in this whole system all over the place. Will it all give way at once? Hard to say, because there are a lot of things propping it up, but there is certainly an evolutionary process that is taking place that is making a lot of changes. They just can't hold us back that much longer.

I think that's right. Maybe something dramatic will happen somewhere, but more likely change will come in little ebbs and flows. There is so much pressure on compulsory schooling, from so many directions, I think there will be little movements, compromises and a lot of backpedalling from schools. And soon enough, schools as we once knew them will be rare.

For example, there are several public schools in the Vancouver area that now incorporate homeschool aspects, allowing kids to do self-paced work, come part time, etcetera, purely because they are desperate to keep their numbers and funding up. At the same time, I'm now hearing of homeschoolers who are being allowed to attend their local schools one or two afternoons a week, which totally contravenes school restrictions but, again, schools are desperate for funding.

That's interesting. Stuff like that just can't happen in New York right now. Specifically, there are similar things happening in other jurisdictions that are very negative. Like in California, where they are setting up public homeschool programs in order to keep those dollars, and then trying to make all the other homeschoolers who won't enroll illegal. Trying to force everyone to homeschool through the public school system. That's one of the things that can happen that is kind of scary.

Sure. Compulsory schooling ain't gonna go easy. They are going to do everything they can to hang on and protect their interests. But why do you have a particular interest in democratic schools?

Because I believe in the process. I think it is the most powerful process among the alternatives, for various reasons. Not only is it important to empower everyone involved, but I think it is a right of students to control their own education. And it is also very, very effective educationally. Even in terms of vocabulary; we had kids in my school that went up six grades in half a year, just because they really wanted to know what was going on, to know what was being discussed.

Is it worth attempting democratic process in a public school?

Sure, as long as you're really clear and honest about what your limitations are, you can have democratic process anywhere. I went into a public at-risk school and got them started with this democratic process. The kids' first reaction was very skeptical, you could tell from their body language, everything, and by the end of the thing they were on the edge of their seats, running for different positions and all. The teachers admitted, though, that they weren't free, that there were a lot of things they couldn't do, couldn't change, but that they'd be willing to go to the school board on some of them. The democratic process changed their whole relationships.

Do you think that public schools can be reformed? Are they worth working with?

Who knows? But I believe in this evolutionary process. There is a group I'm sure you know about, the Separation of School and State, Marshall Fritz's project. I've been to several of their meetings, and my concern with them is that they don't accept the idea of an evolutionary process. And I just don't think that's reality. I think it's not going to happen like that. They don't even like charter schools or vouchers, they think that's still giving the state too much power. The argument that anything that props up public schooling just slows down the inevitable process of change is countered by the argument that every change moves the whole system in the right direction. I don't think there is any clear answer to that question.

In a lot of ways I agree. Answering compulsory schooling has to be a localized thing, dependent on all kinds of unique circumstances, possibilities, predilections and so many other factors. How you go about challenging schools, from what directions, doesn't particularly matter so long as the larger intention is to crack the system. The reality is that there are kids, your kids, in front of you and you have got to build something better, now.

That's right. Here is an example of how democratic process can work, not only in regular school situations. I've set up a democratic structure at the table-tennis club where I volunteer: the kids have complete control of it, and it's amazing how they run the challenge ladder. They have made all the rules, everybody knows all the rules and it just runs like clockwork.

Do you think that all kids would thrive in a democratic school?

Generally, yeah. I think it is really a right. Some may or may not participate, but all kids should have the right.

What do you think of the homeschooling and / or unschooling movement (such as it is)?

I think it is the most powerful force for educational change right now. Because these are people who have gone outside the system, which I really think you have to do to effect change. They can't be controlled the way everyone else, even people in private schools, can be controlled. When anyone threatens them in any way, everyone, the politicians and everyone, are just stunned by the reactions. In Connecticut recently they were discussing changing the way homeschoolers were certified, and they had over a thousand people show up at the hearing, not just local people but folks from all over the place, and they just shot it down.

I think that the kinds of people that are homeschooling right now are as eclectic a group as you could have. It's just such a wide variety of people, and yet the most different kinds of people wind up being able to work together, including groups now that get together the secular and religious homeschoolers.

What do you think the homeschooling movement has to offer the huge number of parents who really shouldn't be with their kids more than is really necessary?

Well, I don't know about that, because there are a lot of kids who call themselves self-schoolers. It's not necessary for parents to be working with their kids all the time. Which is part of the idea behind homeschool resource centres, and I think is really the wave of the future.

There is an obvious limit to the number of homeschoolers, because of parents who are working, or single parents. There are a lot of parents who have managed to get around circumstances, there are ways to do it, but you have to be very creative. I think with a resource centre, that opens much, much greater possibilities.

You are familiar with Ivan Illich's long-held critique of free schools as simply nicer versions of the same disabling institutions that try to treat, or educate, kids while undermining their capacity to drive their own lives. Any comments?

Sure, I just don't buy it. I had lots of similar kinds of discussions with John Holt after he became a full-time homeschool advocate. He came to realize that there was a kind of alternative free school that works the same way, or as well, as homeschooling.

Homeschooling and Homelearning

At some point in the late seventies, early eighties, the alternative independent school movement sort of lost its legs, buried under waves of paleo-conservative backlash, liberal reformism and grim socio-political times. In large part homeschooling has washed in to fill that space, and all that alternative school energy has in part been reconstituted in the homeschooling movement. Over the last twenty or twenty-five years, homeschooling has grown by leaps and bounds, in popularity, in practicality, in legality and in relevance, to the point where even *Time* magazine has put homeschoolers on its cover.

In *Time*'s estimation, in the United States "at least 850,000 students were learning at home in 1999, the most recent year studied; some experts believe the figure is actually twice that . . . In Canada the number of homeschoolers is believed to have increased by four or five times in the past five years."[137]

While there was some satisfaction among homeschoolers that the world had conferred some kind of social respectability upon them, it was widely argued that the numbers were well underestimated, which the magazine made some reference to. At the close of 2002, depending on your sources, there were somewhere between 1.3 and 1.8 million homeschoolers in the U.S. and approximately 70,000 in Canada.[138]

People have all sorts of reasons for not sending their kids to school, the dominant rationale being religious. Many kinds of religious folks do not see secular schools as fitting with their versions of the good life, describing the world as they see it, administering the appropriate discipline or providing the appropriate social milieu. Then there is another whole layer of homeschoolers who believe that schools are not serving their kid's unique needs, be

137. *Time Magazine*, Canadian Edition, August 27, 2001, 41-42.
138. See for example the National Homeschool Education Research Institute <http://www.nheri.org>.

they gifted, specially challenged or unusually inclined. This category might also include a whole loathsome group of homeschoolers who don't want their kids around "different" children of other races, backgrounds or classes. Then there are others who do not believe schools to be effective or efficient enough, and who attempt to improve on the standards at home.

I don't want to talk about any of these homeschoolers here. I'm interested in considering the wide range of homeschoolers who are not attempting to re-create or refine school at home, but are objecting to schools on pedagogical, political, social and / or philosophical reasons: homelearners. These families[139] are open and eager to ask fundamental questions about what they and their children need to thrive and to grow up right, and do not believe schools can provide answers to those questions.

$$\odot \quad \odot \quad \odot$$

In a lot of ways the self-reliant ethic that drives homeschooling and homelearning is very attractive to me. It relies on a do-it-yourself attitude, a refusal to whine to authorities to fix your problems, a willingness to answer to and for yourself and to work with and for your kids. I can only dream about those attributes being so prevalent in a wider society. That said, while I have always supported homeschooling and will continue to do so, much of my personal and political interest in the movement (which it surely is) is inhibited for some very clear reasons. I really do think that homeschooling is a big part of ending compulsory schooling, and at the same time it is a limited ideal.

In large respect, homeschooling is necessarily a middle-class movement. Pulling your kids out of school is a great idea for families that can have a parent at home or available, but what about

---

139. I am using family in the widest possible sense, not at all conveying "two parents, two kids," but a collection of people of various ages who choose to name themselves as such.

single parents who have to work? Or two-parent families that need both parents working? Or immigrant families that badly want their kids to understand a new culture? As a schoolteacher friend said recently, "Almost all my kids are from recently arrived Mexican families. They almost all have two parents who work really long factory hours. They just want their kids to be able to read and write English and get better jobs than they have. Can you imagine talking about homeschooling to them?" No.

I don't want to suggest that it is impossible for single parents, low-income families or recent immigrant families to homeschool their kids. It is absolutely possible, as evidenced by literally thousands of families around the continent — and many in my own neighbourhood — who do not have financial reservoirs and are being sustained by their own energy and desire. It is not that it's impossible, but it's not a realistic option for most people, so homeschooling can only be posed as a limited counterinstitution to compulsory schooling. Limited, but powerful in a lot of ways, and still underestimated all too frequently by its critics.

This is a tough thing to say, but in a lot of ways kids from good, solid families are going to be all right no matter what. Kids who are well-parented, have a relative degree of stability and a minimum of physical or emotional traumas are probably going to get by just fine no matter what their schooling scenario. There are degrees of quality, and certainly real choices that can be made, but in large respect, kids with quality home lives are resilient and supported enough to survive and often thrive almost anywhere. For these kids and families, homeschooling is a wonderful idea, if it can be arranged. It is for all the rest of the kids that the idea starts to break down.

Frankly speaking, many kids I have worked with over the years simply don't want to be around their parents, even from a very young age, and for lots of good reasons. For many, their parents probably shouldn't be around them more than is really necessary either. For a lot of kids, getting to school — even a terrible school — is the safest, funnest, most fulfilling time of their day. Lots of kids, and lots of kids I know, go home to far worse than the worst school can manufacture.

So at that level, it is difficult to see how homeschooling can present itself as a legitimate alternative to those who most need it. Just like beautiful, high-tuition free schools, how can homeschooling be much more than a pleasant middle-class option? And if that option is only really available to kids who already have a world of opportunity, how much does / should it matter? In the case of homeschooling, I think there are some good, if incomplete answers to these questions.

First, the easy characterization of homeschooling as an *exclusively* white, middle-class event is false, and even falser is the assumption that it cannot become more diverse. There is something deeply condescending about the assumption that poor or marginalized families are incapable of pulling their children out of school. While economic stability is certainly helpful, more than anything homeschooling requires a drive and willingness to devote real time and energy to the project. Very often it is the racist assumptions and / or class biases of state schools that drive parents to create something better for their children.

> Homeschooling is empowering. It means taking control and making decisions for one's own family and one's own children instead of abdicating these rights and responsibilities to others or simply complying with societal norms. Particularly for African Americans, schools are by and large failing our children even while they have convinced us that they know best . . . Certainly if we spread the word about this alternative then every Black family could at least consider it, which is the beginning of regaining control and making choices about our children's education.[140]

If it can be said that the homeschooling movement is not a particu-

---

140. Pamela Sparks, "The Daily Rhythm of Life," in Llewellyn, *Freedom Challenge* (Eugene, Ore: Lowry House, 1996), 31.

larly diverse one in some ways, then there is no endemic reason why that needs to be so in the future. There is every reason to believe that homeschooling, conceived as a social project, can become an inclusive tendency.

Similarly, the assessment of homeschooling as *necessarily* individualistic tends to be a reactionary twitch. For those parents who are interested in replicating school at home, homeschooling can certainly become isolating, but there is no reason to describe homeschooling as such. The attempt to re-create school schedules, curricula, methodologies and systems in the home is an absurd project, yet one many families undertake for a variety of reasons, and one that is often very isolating.

The homelearners that I know and have visited in communities across North America, however, do what most parents do almost instinctively: they get together, have a coffee or a smoke and let their kids play and socialize, attend events, build stuff and cause trouble. The homelearners that I know are incredibly social and organize networks and associations and field trips and study groups and conferences constantly. More than anything, home-schoolers rely on one another for support, and the net result is far *less* isolating than being another anonymous family in a mass compulsory system.

There is also a whole new batch of homeschooling centres that are starting to spring up around the continent. Some are resource centres where like-minded parents and kids can gather, some are rented rooms in church basements or community centres, some are scheduled programs and events in homes or parks, some are larger ventures like Pathfinder in Amherst, which is a year-round resource centre for sixty homeschooling teens that offers classes and activities. The idea that homeschooling is necessarily isolating doesn't match up with experience or reality.

Strong homeschooling community networks are often able to support one another, to trade child care, to adjust schedules, to be flexible enough to support single parents or families who want to keep their children out of school and have to maintain employment or other commitments. It is the act of withdrawing from compulsory schooling that tends to stimulate families into becoming active and resourceful community members, into becoming actors, not being acted on.

By conscientiously objecting to or rejecting school, kids and parents regain a tremendous amount of control in their lives that was perceived to have been lost or ceded. The confused and confusing logic of mandatory schooling tends to obscure or degrade the ability of people, both kids and parents, to actively participate in directing their lives. Refusing school often revives the ability of families to engage the larger world, not retreat from it. As David Guterson nicely put it:

> Putting the child at the centre of her education does not put our culture, by extension, on the periphery; on the contrary, it lays the groundwork for successfully bringing the two together, for instilling in her a lifelong thirst for understanding her world.[141]

Not going to school doesn't mean just staying home, it means kids have time and space to engage with the "real world" and design their own lives. One of the most important failings of schools is their insistence on keeping kids segregated with packs of other children their same age throughout their childhood. The ability to build real relationships with people both younger and older than yourself is a critical skill almost totally neglected in schools. Kids who don't go to school tend to play with others around their same age, but almost always are oblivious to obsessive aging of others around them so common in schools. More importantly, kids who are out of school tend to view adults with less suspicion and thus often move more easily in the wider community.

There is no reason that homeschooling parents have to have

141. Guterson, *Why Homeschooling Makes Sense.*

any particular skills or degrees or knowledge to homeschool suc-
cessfully, but there is a degree of confidence or at least moxie
required. There are tremendous social pressures put on kids who
do not go to school, and both parents and kids need to be able to
answer those forces. For families that are self-contained, especially
economically, like farming families for example, many of those
answers are relatively easy. The same is often true of wealthier
families who can pay for a wide range of classes, services, travel
and events and can build an alternative curriculum. For many
other families, though, there is a need for the confidence that
comes with community. Homeschooling networks go a long way
towards providing the stability and support that school-resisting
families rely on, but it is critical in my view to root those networks
in physical communities.

Schooling is a social problem and requires social answers.
Homeschoolers have to be able to answer the inherent elitism of
the movement by developing the kinds of networks and supports
necessary so that it's not just kids from "good" families who can
flourish outside of schools. At some point I think that those problems are simply more than homeschooling alone can solve. The
idea is a lovely one in many ways and possible for a much, much
wider range of kids than is generally understood. The reality of our
culture, though, and certainly the neighbourhood I live and work
in, is that there is a huge number of kids who simply cannot spend
a lot of time at home. There are lots and lots of families that are in
various stages of disrepair, and the kids badly need to get away.
There are innumerable families whose members simply do not get
along, families that need to keep their time together minimized,
that do not have the resources to take care of each other. It is not
good enough to talk about homeschooling with these families.

In the end, I think homeschooling and homelearning are important and necessarily limited. The movement is a major counter-
force to compulsory state schooling and will certainly demand a
bigger role in forging something new. It should be supported at

every step and given every encouragement to become a possibility for all families, and the challenge of homeschooling's inherent elitism should be consciously and constantly engaged by those most committed to its development. Really, homelearners need to take the next step and move from taking good care of their families to taking good care of the community and making it possible for all kids in the neighbourhood to get out of school.

Grace Llewellyn

Grace Llewellyn taught school for three years before unschooling herself and writing The Teenage Liberation Handbook: How to Quit School and Get a Real Life and Education. *Since then, her work has been mostly lumped together under the umbrella of "unschooling advocate." She edited* Real Lives: Eleven Teenagers Who Don't Go to School *and* Freedom Challenge: African American Homeschoolers, *and co-authored, with Amy Silver,* Guerrilla Learning: How to Give Your Kids a Real Education With or Without School. *She's spoken to groups and conferences, given workshops, directed a homeschooling resource centre, produced a mail-order book catalogue, published a newsletter and written articles — all with the purpose of helping people (mostly teenagers) take more control of their own lives and educations. Since 1996 she has directed the annual Not Back to School Camp (now held in both Oregon and West Virginia) for unschooled teenagers and gets her hands into numerous other projects. An enthusiastic belly dance student, performer and teacher, she lives in Oakland, California.*

☉ ☉ ☉

So what's going on for you these days, G-Funk?

I'm working on a book for teenagers who are in conventional school and have no plans to leave. My goal is to encourage them toward a few key paradigm shifts and help them see how they can take greater control over their own learning even within the system. I've wanted to write this book for ten years and made a few false starts. Up until now my other projects have demanded precedence, but I think I'm finally going to be able to focus on it and make it happen.

I am also constantly refining and thinking about and experimenting with Not Back to School Camp — we're heading into our eighth year and recently started a West Virginia camp in addition to our annual Oregon event.

And I'm considering trying again to launch "the Dream House," particularly if I move back to Eugene, Oregon, where I imagine that would be more feasible than where I now live in the San Francisco Bay area. The Dream House was an elaborate idea I had a few years back for a residential house where about sixteen unschooled teenagers would live together for three months at a time, each working on an individual project and learning to live in community and handle basic living skills like cooking, gardening, shopping, etcetera.

Finally, I have the "other" department of my career, in which I belly dance in a Moroccan restaurant. Oh yeah, and I'm fantasizing about learning to do counselling work (psychotherapy and such), but that's another long story!

When you talk to parents and kids these days, what kinds of advice do you tend to offer? Do you recommend that everyone drop out and stay out of school as much as possible?

I'm beginning to listen and speak more broadly than that. I continue to feel that, other things being equal, the best choice for most people would be to rise out of school. For the most part, I feel the same way about all that as when I first wrote the *Teenage Liberation Handbook*. But a key word there is "choice." Choice has to come from within, and if after being presented with the basic case for unschooling (via my book or some equivalent) someone isn't moved to unschool, then I have no incentive to push.

Also, I increasingly see how important it is for parents to psychically, if not materially, support their kids in unschooling. By that I mean more than simply saying, "OK, I guess I'll let you do what you want." If they can't come up with psychic support, that's a serious drawback, bound to undercut the kid's confidence and enthusiasm. I wouldn't tell a kid not to unschool because of it, but if she went ahead, I'd feel some concern and protectiveness toward her and strongly urge her to find an adult willing to put some serious energy into mentoring and encouraging her.

I also feel that ultimately the situation — whether a kid is in school or out — does not determine whether that kid can be happy and fulfilled. Situations, school and any other circumstances we find ourselves in, have a huge impact, but human beings have the power to spin gold out of all kinds of straw. That's the point of my new book.

How do you speak about homeschooling or unschooling to families where both parents work, or to single parents with full-time jobs? What do you say?

Since my work has focused on teenagers, this isn't an issue that I've had to address a whole lot. The kind of unschooling that I encourage teenagers to do really isn't at all dependent on having parents around full time. If family relationships are good then, sure, it's nice for one parent to be at home, emotionally and physically accessible. But a teenager can meet much of his need for adult guidance through other people, drawing on parents' wisdom and support as they are available.

Believe me, though, I think about this issue a lot when I try to squint into my own personal crystal ball. I'm single and I very much want to have kids. And I'm thirty-eight so I don't see myself waiting around to find a partner, so I anticipate coming up hard against the conflict between wanting to nurture my kids (particularly when they're really young) versus wanting and needing to work. I have lots of strategies in mind, and yes, the possibilities do include part-time enrollment in a carefully chosen school. There are so many working parents, now, who make unschooling work through some combination of serendipity, devotion and brilliant organization and planning that I'm convinced I will be OK.

Is homeschooling essentially a middle-class movement? Is it limited to that?

From what I've witnessed, yes, the vast majority of homeschoolers are middle class. And white. But one, the movement is large. So while the percentage of non-white homeschoolers is small, and the percentage of working-class homeschoolers probably even smaller, there is still a large number of these folks. I think we often don't see them at homeschooling events; sometimes they tend to be even more do-it-yourself than the rest of the movement. Do you know about the Self-Education Foundation? They tend to know about, and support, some of these sub-communities.

Two, this isn't an original observation, but I agree with whoever said it first: a very large percentage of homeschooling parents are themselves of a middle-class background, but they have chosen to live without many of the trappings of a middle-class life. In other words, it is likely that only one parent works, and perhaps at a career that provides more satisfaction than money. They may have themselves chosen not to graduate from college. Lots of back-to-the-landers, cultural creatives, artists, voluntary simplicity folks — I think a high proportion of homeschoolers fall into these and similar categories. And while that doesn't change their class background, they're not the people that we first see in our minds' eyes when we hear the term "middle class."

Finally, three, I don't at *all* see any good reason why working-class folks couldn't and shouldn't be unschooling. As a group, they've been more harmed by schools — the system tends to preserve the status quo — and thus, I think, have more to gain by getting out. People are quick to say, "But homeschooling takes money." It doesn't, though. Not much. Money, used wisely, can be a significant benefit, but what homeschooling takes is initiative and confidence, a willingness to ask for help and to negotiate trades, and knowledge of and some sense of entitlement to a share in public resources — libraries, wildernesses, etcetera. Class backgrounds, of course, mean not only money, but also a subculture with its own mentality. Confidence in things perceived "educational" may not be one of the strengths of the working class, and I think that's the biggest barrier.

I notice that some unschooled kids that I work with occasionally have difficulty in situations that require sacrifice and discipline. Now that's hardly just unschoolers, but after spending much or most of their youth doing what they want, following their own interests and rejecting circumstances that they find boring or oppressive, they sometimes have trouble adjusting in scenarios that are less than ideal: jobs, college, training, whatever. Not always, obviously, and I wouldn't say that of all the unschoolers I know, but sometimes I think that, and maybe that's a good thing. One of the things school teaches (or at least taught me) is how to adapt and cope with challenging, oppressive, ugly situations and come out OK. Comments?

Yeah . . . well, first of all, I've certainly observed both extremes and everything in between in unschoolers. Like, I'm thinking in this moment of an eighteen-year-old woman who quit school about five years ago. She is the youngest member of a professional marimba band, and she got her pilot's licence about a year ago and is about to start teaching people to fly. Plus, she's extremely sweet and friendly and a good friend to many people.

As for unschoolers having difficulty in situations that require sacrifice and discipline, I'm with you. Sometimes this is a good thing; when the situation is oppressive or meaningless, as many jobs and school situations are, I'm not sure that "sacrifice" or "discipline" are healthy responses. But I would like to see us, as a community, support young people in consciously examining these situations and then making more clear, conscious choices as to the responses they want to make. Do they want to remove themselves from a particular situation and find a situation that they find worthy of their dedication? Do they want to find a way to change their situation so that they feel good about staying in it? Or does it seem that, all things considered, this is the best or the only option available to them at this time, and accept that and find a way to maintain their personal integrity within the situation? What I don't want us to encourage is a victim mentality, where someone stays in a situation but complains about it or avoids facing it. That's potentially one of the best things about a teenager leaving school — instead of doing the passive "well, I hate school but I have to do it" thing, she's saying, "I don't like this situation and instead of complaining and feeling sorry for myself, I'm going to get out and take responsibility for my own growth and happiness."

I may be idealistic, but I don't think that any young person needs to settle for a bad overall situation. Of course, though, all of us need to make sacrifices and develop discipline in service of that which we believe in and feel passionate about. To the degree that I observe unschoolers avoiding this — and, honestly, it's not a lot — I want us to encourage them past that. That may mean, first, supporting them in articulating just what it is that they deem worthy of their love, their energy, their hard work — and yes, their sacrifice and discipline.

Part of the rationale for mass compulsory schooling is that schools perform a certain amount of social levelling. That is, all kids, from whatever background, can get similar (if not the same) opportunities, and a collective culture can be forged. If independent schools, homeschooling and deschooling proliferate, won't our society degenerate into an every-person-for-

themselves, individualistic thing? How can unschooling be something more than just an individualistic ethic?

It seems to me that most of the homeschoolers I know are community-building people who are creating more interdependence, not less. And I don't mean just within the homeschooling community. Many homeschoolers are active in their local schools — they volunteer or help with fundraisers or special events. Others aren't, of course — some in our community are pretty isolated.

In a way I feel surprised by this question every time I hear a version of it, because overall I think unschoolers tend to experience themselves as part of the larger human community more than schoolers do. When you're in school, so much of your energy goes into figuring out who you're with and who you're against or is against you. And despite all the wishful and sloppy thinking on this issue, schools are much more about sorting kids into winners and losers, and hardening the lines between these groups, than about any kind of equal opportunity. When you're unschooling, good chance you're doing some kind of volunteer work, good chance the people you have positive relationships with represent a wide range of ages, good chance you're learning both to give and to receive, rather than to obey and to passively accept what you're given. I think all of this is good for society.

And, at the same time, I don't want to dismiss these concerns . . . it all depends on the individual and on the individual family. Both their positive and negative qualities may play out more fully than schooling folks' attributes do, since they have more power over the educational process. If a homeschooling family has a fearful or arrogant window on the world, then yes, their actions will contribute to division amongst people — probably more than if their kids were in school. But if a homeschooling family seeks to be a contributing and gratefully receiving part of the larger community, then there, too, they have greater power to do so than a schooling family does.

Deschooling: Alternatives to School

I am trying to build an argument and describe a scenario in which compulsory state schooling can be disassembled from multiple directions. I do not think that school can or should be replaced by another *system*, nor are any of these pieces answers on their own. It is exactly the attempt to build a universal system that has got us where we are now. Compulsory schooling shouldn't be replaced, it should be deconstructed, if you'll excuse the cheap analogy, very much like the Berlin Wall. Not by legislation or by a major government initiative, but by thousands of people with hammers, ripping the thing up with their hands.

My contention here is that the best of those hammers include, but are not limited to, hijacking public schools, building independent alternatives and homeschooling. I've looked quickly at all three of these approaches, saying good things and offering serious critiques of each. I both support and have real reservations about all three, and now I want to talk about deschooling, the best name I have to describe where most of my faith and energy around schooling is located.

I love many free schools and their vision and heart. I totally admire the people who work and run them, and the families who are willing to build a better place. I have much respect for homeschoolers and especially those homelearners who are not just looking out for themselves. I love that so many families are simply pulling their kids out of school and figuring it out themselves. And still I have some real doubts and concerns that democratic schools and homeschooling are just not getting to the root of the problem. It is not the character or content of schools that is the real problem; it is the fundamental conception of schooling itself.

Ivan Illich has described the idea of education as very close to original sin, except that people are born tainted by original ignorance and have to be treated by specialized services or institutions to save them from themselves. Illich has long argued that free schools are another disabling institution, attempting to create good people and mould citizens, reflexively arrogant in the assumption of their place as arbiters of the good life. In the end, perhaps all schools are manipulative, whether they are overtly obnoxious or relatively pleasant, and undermine the ability of people to genuinely run their own lives.

There is something essential there, and the best of free schools are engaged with the critique and able to respond. There is something there, though, that is extremely tough to address for people who have put their lives and hearts into creating innovative schools.

I tend to believe that while alternative schools are of real and definite value, what is most needed are *alternatives to school*, and that the best institutions are actively attempting to become that.

A good place to start is with what might be called a utility model. The best public institutions, those that are universally admired and non-manipulative, are those that do not attempt to mould their users. Libraries, parks, public swimming pools, community centres and playgrounds are all great examples of public utilities. They are paid for with public funds, are free or cheap for everyone to use, and are open for groups or individuals to use as tools.

Contemporary libraries are a great example of what schools might become. They are indispensable supports of intellectual activity, they have a huge variety of resources from books to Internet services to compact discs to helpful librarians to sophisticated research databases to public lectures. Libraries are equally useful to small children and adults of all ages, whether you are interested in classical music, organizational theory, boat building, boxing or anything else. They are open early, late and weekends, accept everyone, are responsive to community needs and make no specific demands on users' time.

It doesn't take a great leap of imagination to see how schools, with their incredible resources, huge staffs full of eager and talented people, massive budgets, gyms, science equipment, books, computers and everything else might one day become equally valuable community resources. I have heard Helen Hughes speak of developing a "learnery," and the idea that schools can adapt to emulate libraries is a very attractive one to me.

I think the entire construction, not just of compulsory schooling but also the fundamental assumption of schooling's exigency, needs to be chucked and totally reimagined. Which, I acknowledge as I write, may be close to impossible because our entire culture has been so obsessively schooled to believe that only professional treatment can make us the people we want to be. All of our assumptions about how children should be growing up need to be carefully turned and turned again.

Someone who worked with a small free school once told me that at the end of every school year they burned their book of rules and regulations so that at the beginning of every year they could build a new set of rules with a new set of kids and families. A nice idea and gesture, and the funny thing, he said, was at the end of every year the book had pretty much the same set of rules. Similarly, it is often rightly said that if schools were simply decompulsorized, if it was immediately the case that children were not required to go, probably the schools would fill up the next day with little change.

In some ways, in the context of everyday living, my desire to rethink everything is the kind of idle foolishness that academics are so fluent in. I have young kids, you might well have kids, we all have lives and work that we want to do, big plans, and our children want and need many things every day. Our kids want places to go, friends to hang out with, convivial spaces where they can play, fun projects to take part in and their energy and enthusiasm for the world demand replies every day.

It is of questionable value to parents or kids to suggest we sit down and start the whole deal over, because life goes on and our children are growing up as we talk here. And yet, there really is value in imagining a better world — not just vicarious psychological pleasure, but real political and lived value. There is only one chance for our kids to be kids. When are we going to end the absurdity of schooling and use all that money and resources and good people and good intentions to do something better?

I think it wholly possible to reinvent the whole thing en route, to build the road as we travel,[142] to consider in local, specific context what the kids around us need and want to grow up well. Play? Work? Academics? Classes? What size of groups? What kinds of spaces? All of it. And then go from there, acting not on pedagogy or dogmatism, but on the lived experience of the world around us. It may sound crazed, but really it is what parents do every day with their children and have always done. Parents sit down with not much to go on except the collective cultural experiences surrounding them, and try to bring a child up well. Millions and millions of parents do incredibly well figuring it out as they go, not turning their kids over to experts for treatment, but relying on themselves and their family, friends and community. I think it is this experience of family and extended family that can be enlarged further to the larger community, that makes real sense in building alternatives to school.

◎ ◎ ◎

I want to describe a little project we are running here in East Vancouver because I think it demonstrates what can be done in a poor community with few resources. I think it illustrates how possible it is to build counterinstitutions and describe them in the most optimistic and hopeful ways.

I have been running a non-profit society, called the Purple Thistle Community Society, in the city since 1992. It is the funnel through which all of the youth and community projects I develop

142. To steal a good phrase from Spain's Mondragon system of co-operatives, also the title of Roy Morrison's book about them.

can be run. After all these years, as many of the kids we have been doing stuff with have gotten older, we noticed that what we really wanted and needed was space in the neighbourhood where youth could hang out, be creative, focus youth-driven projects, meet with mentors and many other things.[143]

In November of 2001, seven teenaged friends and I began meeting regularly, trying to figure out what such a centre might look like. We batted around ideas for many weeks, talking about maybe a café or a warehouse, or maybe studio space or attaching ourselves to an existing project. We came up with all kinds of good plans and really had no money to make any of them work.

East Vancouver, specifically the Commercial Drive neighbourhood where we live, is a genuinely wonderful place. It is poor, diverse, funky, full of activists and artists, there are cafés and public places everywhere, and to my mind a lot seems possible. It is also burdened by high rents, predatory landlords, really low vacancy rates and onerous municipal regulations. Considering what kind of centre we wanted to run meant in large respect figuring out what kind of space we could get into and what we could get past the city. It is kind of an ass-backwards way to start a place, but it is reality.

We had no money at all until we ran into a youth grant from a large local foundation, which bought our idea of a different kind of youth centre and gave us a little more than seventeen grand to get going with. We were thrilled and almost immediately lucked into a great office space. It was pretty beat up, which helped us get a decent break on the rent in return for renovations, and it was zoned in a way that I was able to slide it past the city planning and permit departments.

The Purple Thistle Centre is not a big or elaborate place in any way: four big rooms with a mini-kitchen area and a darkroom we

---

143. We interpret youth here to mean folks between the ages of fifteen and twenty-three, although we are hardly rigorous about it.

built ourselves, on the second floor of a nondescript building above a video store. It has good light, great views of the city and, best of all, it is right in the heart of our neighbourhood, overlooking the park and community centre. In all it is as good a place as we could have hoped for. The eight of us spent about a month and a half cleaning it up, painting, fixing stuff and refinishing the floors.

By May the place was looking great, except we weren't ready at all. The grant and space had come through quite suddenly, and we really weren't prepared. We were all ready to open our doors, but had little solid plan of action, absolutely no money to work with (our initial grant was just enough to cover rent and utilities for a year, nothing more), no programs, no furniture, no gear and only a few concrete projects on the go. On top of that I was leaving town for all of July to lecture, and then the whole bunch of us were going up north in August (more on that in a minute). It was both exciting and dismaying and highly questionable if we could pull it off.

Since then, a little more than a year after we opened our doors, the thing is coming together beautifully. Our collective that is running the centre has spent a lot of time talking through ideas, learning what is realistic and what exactly we are after. We are only occasionally close to grasping either of these, but we are doing a lot of good things, and I think something pretty compelling is emerging.

⊘   ⊘   ⊘

We started with broad categories of activities that the kids, their friends and colleagues are most excited by: art, writing, social activism, music, photography, film and videography, graphic design, web design, bike building, songwriting and travel.[144] We have iden-

---

144. The kids involved (around fifty right now) are pretty much all from the east side of Vancouver, though youths come from every part of the Lower Mainland and overwhelmingly come from low-income families. Some are in school, some are not, some are homeless, some attend colleges, quite a few have part-time jobs and very many are what others would call "at risk."

tified all of these as key components of what we want to have happen here and are developing projects in each category as it becomes possible. We pull together collections of youth into specific working groups of between ten and fifteen kids in each of these areas, hooking them up with local mentors and then collaboratively developing community projects. Everything is free, from the cameras and darkroom space to community art projects to camping trips to exchanges to magazine publishing to various classes, and the groups all continue to thrive and develop.

Our visual arts group, for example, meets weekly, building the group, developing skills and working on a series of projects for a couple of different places in the neighbourhood. The next step for the art group is putting together a major art piece in collaboration with the local community centre, which involves fundraising, community outreach, planning and organizing the work, on top of actually producing the piece. The writing group is operating with a similar trajectory, developing a youth magazine (*Ritalin: medicate yourself*) piece by piece, with all the steps that entails, and publishing smaller zines frequently. We also spend a lot of time reaching out to other youth and community groups in the neighbourhood to work with us on various projects.

One of the key parts of the centre's mandate is travel. Every year for a decade now I have taken big groups of kids on long excursions. This means taking up to twenty-five teens, as well as my two young daughters, camping for a month at a time, including trips to Death Valley in California, throughout Montana, Nevada, the canyon lands of Utah and through Alberta. Three adults (me, Selena and our buddy Rich) were there to drive the vans, advise the kids and watch over the general organization, but for the entire trip the kids had to do all their own shopping, cooking, cleaning, tenting and packing. The trips are designed to challenge the kids, to develop their independence and self-reliance, and test their basic capacity to care for themselves.

What we have all noticed over the years is that while the participants all gain good doses of confidence in their own abilities, it is the collective experiences that are really central. In travelling together for long stretches, sometimes in trying circumstances, the groups come together and the kids learn to trust and rely on one another in ways that they might never have guessed. In many ways, these trips have been really key in drawing together and energizing the larger group of kids I work with, and as we have been designing the centre, everyone has emphasized the importance of travelling together.

This past year we decided to try something a little different. I had always wanted to run an exchange[145] and had always been equally interested in going to the North. An old friend, Mark Douglas, had recently returned from Fort Good Hope in the Northwest Territories (where he had spent some of his youth), and after talking about the condition of that community and the prospects facing Native youth in the North, we started talking about bringing the kids from the two places together. After about nine months of organizing, working with the chief, community economic development officer and youth worker in Fort Good Hope, and fundraising for the amazingly high travel expenses, we managed to pull it off.

The trip was an incredible one in a lot of ways, and plenty of work. We took twelve kids and two adults north, with a similar number[146] coming south, each for ten days at a stretch. The two places could hardly have been more different within Canada: one a multicultural, urban neighbourhood in Vancouver, the other an isolated Dene settlement on the Mackenzie River, 20 kilometres south of the Arctic Circle. Television, though, has had an amazing effect on isolated communities: everyone has satellite dishes, the

145. I participated in an exchange program to India when I was a teenager and it made an indelible mark on my life.
146. The Fort Good Hope group was short two youths, both of whom were chucked in jail while we were there and were unable to travel.

kids are covered in hip-hop gear and their virtual exposure to southern culture is constant.

The central focus of the project was dealing with racism face to face. Kids are bombarded with anti-racism messages, largely through school and the media, and yet often have little chance to deal with racism in an immediate and visceral way. The core of the exchange was about learning how to appreciate, communicate, live and travel with people who are very different from oneself, and how to comprehend and value their culture and home lives.

The kids were billeted with each others' families,[147] and we attempted to give each other a realistic view of our communities. We happened to drop into Fort Good Hope for a major music and dance festival (which was amazing); we hunted, fished, camped and rode up and down the river. We ate an incredible amount of fresh game. We shot rifles, hauled huge fish out of nets and stayed up all night with the sun. Down south we hiked through the forest, climbed the North Shore mountains, wandered around China-town, went to the beach often and shopped at more malls than we had ever been in before.

The trip was a genuine challenge, in many ways, for everyone involved and drew us together in a fashion that is hard to articulate but most everyone has felt at one time. The desire to travel, to explore almost anywhere else, seems to be a constant among the youth that I work with, and it just has to be a central part of the centre. We have two more trips planned for the coming year, including another exchange with Fort Good Hope, this time in the late fall, and have several more travel ideas incubating.

It is sometimes hard to describe what we want the centre to become; something like a community centre, something like a college, something like a library. The best name we have come up with is ASS (alternative or supplement to school), but that

147. Many of the families in Fort Good Hope were unprepared to have guests stay, so about half of us stayed in a common house.

acronym really isn't very grant-writing / fundraising-friendly. It is an accurate description in a lot of ways though.

The place is open most days and nights, there is always food available and it has a homey feel to it.[148] We have some pretty good computer gear, run various classes and workshops (from Spanish to sexual health), help kids find employment and training spots, have a great schedule of activities and there is a convivial, busy energy throughout the week. We all have more ideas and projects in mind than we can reasonably act on. More than anything, we want to make it possible for kids to build their lives, act on their politics, travel, gain skills, find jobs, work in community and do it without school.

In response to a number of requests, I have actually organized for kids to be able to complete their Grade 10, 11 or 12 through the centre in affiliation with the local adult learning centre. No one has taken me up on the possibility though, maybe because my heart simply isn't in it and I actively discourage kids from finishing their high school. Unless people are really eager, can articulate a good reason for doing high school and can explain why they need to complete the curriculum, I just can't see it. I am very interested in kids going to college and university, but going to high school is not a prerequisite for either. Every college in British Columbia accepts students of nineteen years and older regardless of their academic background, including into university transfer programs, and universities all have mature student policies. There is simply so much possibility, so much exciting, important, intellectually stimulating stuff for kids to do that I cannot see encouraging people to spend their youth on high school. Nevertheless, that option exists through the Purple Thistle.

One of the funny things about running a project like this with youth is a built-in design flaw: as the kids get older and thrive, they

148. Thanks to the many folks who donated chairs and couches, tables and shelves, all our kitchen, desks, rugs, lamps and everything else.

want to get out in the world. The kids that are doing well leave for jobs, travel, college, volunteer projects. The seven original kids who started the centre together all spend major parts of the year away. All are still deeply involved in the project when they are in town, but replacing them is not easy. The original group was fantastic, worked well together, endured plenty of skepticism about our ideas and have really made this happen. New kids are always stepping up to take their place, but it is both wonderful and tough to see them move on.

Sitting here now, the centre really feels a lot like what we imagined, and the reality is that its financial situation remains tenuous but is improving remarkably. It is the fate of all non-governmental projects that are not backed by churches or synagogues or mosques or generous rich people.[149] I remain driven, however, by the possibilities of the centre, and the vision of a real alternative to school.[150] The numbers of kids that keep coming, their eagerness, their enthusiasm and their willingness to get involved in all kinds of projects is what is really sustaining.

◎ ◎ ◎

I am not posing the Purple Thistle Centre as a model for anyone to emulate particularly. It is one response to a complex arrangement of circumstance, desire, personalities, location and time. It is what we have figured out together in this place. The story may hold some inspiration or use for other groups, but really I want to illustrate what is possible.

I think that the range of possibilities in building alternatives to school is virtually boundless, and in different locales, in different

---

149. I try to keep Ben Franklin in mind: "They who trade independence for security will, in the end, deserve neither."

150. You should feel free to call, write or visit us: Purple Thistle Centre, 3-1163 Commercial Drive, Vancouver, B.C., V5L 3X3, 604-255-2838, http://www.purplethistle.org; e-mail: ptproject@yahoo.com.

neighbourhoods, ways to gather kids may look very different from one another. Released from the burden of schooled expectations, the world opens up for youth and adults alike. When people begin to really address the questions of what it takes for kids, for all of us, to grow up right, the answers are all over the place, and that's nothing but goodness.

My faith lies in small groups of people gathering together and thinking these things through in the context of community. I believe that in the threads of homelearning, democratic schooling, free schools and unschooling there is the raw material, the theoretical and experiential material, to build better places. New institutions do not have to be one or the other of these, or conform to any particular criteria. The best new projects to my mind are those that blur ideological lines, that incorporate disparate elements and build alternatives to school based on everyday lived lives.

Index